The

E-BUSINESS

Dictionary

EDI, E-Procurement, and Supply Chain Terminology.

By Alec Nevalainen
Rockbend Books

TRADEMARKS AND COPYRIGHT

The publisher offers discounts on this book when ordered in quantity for special sales. For more information, please contact sales@rockbend.com.

ISBN 0-9713203-2-2

First Edition: February 2003

10 9 8 7 6 5 4 3 2 1

PREFACE

The E-Business Dictionary: EDI, E-Procurement, and Supply-Chain Terminology, First Edition contains short, clear explanations of words that an average professional might use or encounter in a day-to-day work environment. Types of terms and definitions include technical, business, buzzwords, jargon, slang, and foreign words. I've made a sincere attempt to simplify otherwise long and technical definitions into language that could be understood by people with varying technical and business backgrounds. This edition does not contain full technical specifications, only simplified terms and definitions.

I make no assumption that this edition is complete, and errors and omissions will be found. Updates and revisions can be made at my publisher's website located on the Trademark page. I appreciate all feedback, and will make an effort to implement changes in future editions.

This dictionary is intended for all audiences. Although the front cover indicates "managers, consultants, developers, and salespersons," certainly someone from any background can understand the terms and definitions presented.

The aim, in short, is to provide a complete reference guide to be used sporadically. The reader should find The E-Business Dictionary to be authoritative, clear, and easy to use.

Special thanks to Rob Varnon and Laura Kennedy for their editing help. Also to Paula McGinley for contributions made to the cover design.

A.N.
February 2003

Aa

AAA server *n.* An AAA server is a program that handles requests for access to computer resources. For example, in an enterprise, it provides authentication, authorization, and accounting (AAA) services. The AAA server typically interacts with databases and directories containing user information.

absolute cost advantage *n.* The cost advantage of certain countries in producing certain goods, compared to costs in other countries. The costs of producing similar products vary between different countries because certain resources, such as labor, raw materials, and energy, will be cheaper in some countries than in others. Global enterprises have the ability to take advantage of these cost differences by buying components or products from countries that have these advantages. For example, a shoe manufacturer in an economy with high labor costs may purchase certain components from another country with significantly lower labor costs.

acceptance *v.* The act of accepting by an authorized representative; an indication of a willingness to pay; the assumption of a legal obligation by a party to the terms and conditions of a contract.

acceptance credit *n.* A way of financing the sale of goods, particularly in global trade. It involves a commercial bank or merchant bank extending credit to a foreign importer, whom it sees as creditworthy. In return for this service the exporter pays the bank a fee known as an acceptance commission.

access control *n.* Set of software mechanisms that limit and control access to host systems and applications. Most financial applications use an access control list to designate roles within the organization. For example, managers generally have unlimited access to resources and documents relating to the entire organization whereas computer programmers may only have access to documents relating to their current project.

access control list *n.* A list of users and their permitted access rights. See access control.

accounting code *n.* A multi-segment number that identifies the business unit (division, department, project, etc.) or account to be billed for an order or specific line items on an order. Also known as a cost code, cost center, expenditure code, and income code.

An accounting code sequence includes multiple segments, each of which provides financial information that is important to track. An accounting code segment might represent the following:

- A cost center (such as department or section of an organization)
- An expense code (such as office supplies, maintenance, or professional services)
- A project code, or some other useful category (such as country or region).

Often, accounting code segments defined in an E-Business system is the same as the segments defined in an organization's general ledger financial system.

An organization's legacy ERP system such as SAP or Oracle Financial's

CONTENTS

ARRANGEMENT OF ENTRIES

All main entries are in bold type and arranged in a single alphabetical listing including abbreviations, acronyms, foreign words, and combined forms.

Most entries in this dictionary begin with a lowercase letter. Some entries begin with an uppercase letter, which indicates that the word is usually capitalized.

The part of speech is shown by an abbreviation in italic's placed after the main entry word. All listed parts of speech in this edition include:

adj.	adjective
adv.	adverb
conj.	conjunction
def.art	definite article
indef.art	indefinite article
interj.	interjection
n.	noun
prep.	preposition
pron.	pronoun
v.	verb

Example sentences are shown in italic's; certain common expressions appear in bold italic typeface within examples.

The pronunciation of some words is shown immediately after the main entry. In most words, however, the pronunciation is not shown because it's obvious and commonly used.

may have a complete set of accounting codes that may be considered the "master set" for an E-Business application to draw from. A common task for legacy integration with a new application is making sure there is data integrity between these two systems. In some cases, these systems will do a daily transfer of accounting code updates to ensure this integrity.

account rendered *n*. An unpaid balance appearing in a statement of account, details of which have been given in a previous statement.

accounts payable *n*. The amounts owed by a business to suppliers. Accounts payable are classified as current liabilities on the balance sheet.

accrual *n*. An estimate of a liability that is not supported by an invoice or a request for payment at the time the accounts are prepared. An example of an accrual would be telephone expenses, which are billed quarterly. At the end of the accounting period, if no bill has been received, and estimate (based on past bills) would be made and credited to an accruals account. Also known as accrued charge, accrued expense, accrued liability.

acquisition *v*. The act of acquiring goods and services (including construction) for the use of an organizational activity through purchase, rent, or lease. Includes the establishment of needs, description of requirements, selection of procurement method, selection of sources, solicitation of procurement, solicitation for offers, award of contract, financing, contraction administration, and related functions.

acquisition planning *v*. The process by which the efforts of all personnel responsible for an E-Business application are coordinated and integrated through a comprehensive plan for fulfilling an agency's needs in a timely manner and at a reasonable cost. It includes developing an overall acquisition strategy for managing the acquisition plan.

Acrobat *n.* A program from Adobe that lets you capture a document and then view it in its original format and appearance. Acrobat is ideal for making documents or brochures that were designed for the print medium viewable electronically and capable of being shared with others on the Internet. The Acrobat document format is called a Portable Document Format (pdf) file, you at least need the Acrobat Reader to view pdf's. The Reader is free and can be downloaded from Adobe. You can use it as a standalone reader or as a plug-in in a Web browser.

Active Directory *n.* Active Directory is Microsoft's directory service, a part of the Window's 2000 architecture. Like other directory services, such as Sun One's LDAP Directory Server, Active Directory is a centralized and standardized system that automates network management of user data, security, and directory resources, and enables interoperation with other directories. Active Directory is designed especially for distributed networking environments.

Active Server Page (ASP) *n.* An html page that includes one or more small embedded scripts that are processed on Microsoft's IIS web server before the page is sent to the user. This process is similar to a server-side include or CGI program. A typical usage of ASP involves a user request to a database, producing a dynamic unique process, and the web server builds or customizes the page before sending it to the requestor. Because the processing is done on the server side, any web browser can handle these types of pages. A user knows if they're accessing an Active Server Page if the address in their URL field ends with the '.asp' extension (e.g. http://www.microsoft.com/login.asp).

ActiveX *n.* A set of object-oriented programming technologies and tools developed by Microsoft. It centers on the Component Object Model (COM), and when used in a network with a directory and additional support COM becomes the Distributed Component Object Model (DCOM) which supports the "run-anywhere" model. The main thing that you create when writing a program to run in the ActiveX environment is a component, which is also known as an ActiveX control. ActiveX is Microsoft's response to the Java technology from Sun Microsystems and is roughly equivalent to a Java applet.

activity-based costing (ABC) *n.* An accounting method that enables a business to better understand how and where it makes a profit.

actuals *n.* Commodities that can be purchased and used, rather than goods traded on a futures contract, which are represented by documents.

add-on *n.* An add-on is either a piece of hardware that can be added to a computer to increase its capabilities or a program utility that enhances a primary program. Examples of add-ons include sound cards, graphics acceleration, modem cards, and memory. Software add-ons are common for large servers and personal computers. A plug-in is a similar term originated by Netscape which is a application program that can be activated with a Netscape web browser window.

addendum *n.* An addition or supplement to a document; e.g., items or information added to a procurement document.

additional information field (AIF) *n.* An additional field on a requisition or purchase order line item.

Administrative Management Domain (ADMD) *n.* An X.400 Message Handling Service managed by a common public administrative authority, such as a telephone company, or by a messaging service provider.

adoption process *n.* The mental and behavioral stages through which an individual passes before making a purchase or placing an order. The stages are awareness, interest, evaluation, trial, and finally adoption of the product or service. For example, a company may implement an adoption process when implementing an E-Procurement application.

ADSL *n.* An acronym for Asymmetric Digital Subscriber Line; technology for transmitting digital information at high speeds on existing phone lines in homes and businesses. Unlike regular phone connections, ADSL provides a constant connection to the network (internet). ADSL is very attractive because it also simultaneously accommodates analog (voice) information on the same line. ADSL originally came out in 1996 but achieved mainstream usage in 1998. Currently, ADSL and cable-modem services are competing with each other for the high bandwidth consumer and business markets.

Advanced Encryption Standard (AES) *n.* An encryption algorithm for securing sensitive unclassified material by US Government agencies and may eventually become the standard for commercial transactions in the private sector. Several other encryption standards exist including Data Encryption Standard (DES), and Triple DES. An industry accepted standard is still being debated by standards organizations and will likely be a compromise between DES and triple DES (similar to what AES is now).

advanced planning and scheduling (APS) *n.* A software platform that extends and enhances the data within an ERP system. An APS system can advise an organization on resource and production planning, along with forecasting shifts in production.

advanced shipping notice (ASN) *n.* Electronic notification sent to a buyer organization that confirms shipment of an order. Large vendors sometimes use ASN information to schedule their receiving processes and assess substantial penalties if the supplier fails to send the ASN, or even if it contains incorrect information that changes the dock scheduling.

advertise *v.* To make a public announcement of the intention to purchase goods, services or construction with the intention of increasing the response and enlarging the competition. The announcement must conform to the legal requirements imposed by established laws, rules, policies and procedures to inform the public. Also known as a bid notice.

advertising allowance *n.* A price concession given by a manufacturer of a product to a retailer to allow him to pay for local advertising. It is an effective way of advertising both the product and the retail outlet.

advice note *n.* A note sent to the customer by a supplier of goods to advise him that an order has been fulfilled. The advice note may either accompany the goods or be sent separately, thus preceding the invoice and any delivery note.

Afghani *n.* The standard monetary unit of Afghanistan; its three character currency code is 'AFA'.

afloat *adj.* Marking goods, especially commodities, that are on a ship from their port of origin to a specified port of destination; for example, "afloat Miami" means the goods are on their way to Miami.

after date *n.* The words used in a bill of exchange to indicate that the period of the bill should start from the date inserted on the bill; for example, "30 days after date, we promise to pay x amount".

aggregation *v.* To gather parts and make into a whole. In E-Business, the term is used to indicate the process of bringing buyers and sellers together onto one hub or exchange.

aggregator *n.* Any device that serves multiple devices or by using its own capabilities is able to forward transmissions in a more concentrated and economical way. An example of an aggregator is the remote-access

---

hub, which handles incoming dial-up calls, Integrated Services Digital Network (ISDN) connections, frame-relay traffic while also functioning as a router.

AIAG *n.* Automotive Industry Action Group. This group defines automotive EDI standards.

AIM *n.* Acronym for AOL Instant Messenger; a free instant messaging application provided by America Online. Users are able to set-up 'Buddy Lists' to communicate easily with friends, colleagues, and family. One of the attractive features of instant messaging applications is the lack of a paper trail (or electronic trail in this sense), whereas email is replaced as a means to communicate.

algorithm *n.* A set of well-defined rules for solving a problem in a finite number of steps. Algorithms are extensively used in computer science (E-Business applications). The steps in the algorithm are translated into a series of instructions that the computer can understand. These instructions form the computer program.

allocated quantity *n.* A quantity of an item held in stock that has already been allocated to an end use and is not therefore available to meet other requirements.

allowance 1. *n.* A deduction from an invoice for a specified purpose, such as substandard quality of goods, late delivery, etc. 2. *n.* A price reduction or rebate given to a customer on a large order or for some other specific reason. 3. *n.* An agreed time used in work measurement; it is added to the basic time in calculating the standard time for a particular job. The allowances provide time for rest, relaxation, and other personal needs for workers (toilet breaks).

alphanumeric *adj.* An adjective describing letters or digits, or a combination, and sometimes includes control characters, spaces, and other special characters.

alternate response *n.* A substitute response; an intentional substantive variation to a basic provision or clause of a solicitation by a vendor.

alternative evaluation *n.* A stage in the process of making a purchase in which a buyer uses relevant information to evaluate available alternative brands.

AMD *n.* The second largest maker of personal computer microprocessors after Intel, they also produce flash memory, integrated circuits for networking devices, and programmable logic devices. AMD delivered the Athlon processor in mid 1999 with positive consumer sales. Recently, they announced the first 1-gigahertz PC microprocessor in a new version of the Athlon. Because of increased competition in the microprocessor market (largely due to AMD) PC prices have dropped dramatically during the late 1990's and early 2000.

amendment/change order *n.* A written modification to a contract or purchase order or other agreements.

American National Standards Institute (ANSI) *n.* The organization that develops, oversees and publishes standards in the United States, and represents the United States on the International Standards Organization.

American Registry of Internet Numbers (ARIN) *n.* An organization in the US that manages IP address numbers for the US and other assigned territories. Because these addresses must be unique and because address space on the internet is limited, there is a need for an organization to control and allocate address number blocks. IP number management was formerly a responsibility of the Internet Assigned Numbers Authority (IANA), which contracted to Network Solutions for the actual services. In 1997, this responsibility was turned over to ARIN. When Internet Protocol Version 6 is released, which extends the length of an address from 32 bits to 128 bits, ARIN will have more addresses to manage and allocate.

American Standard Code for Information Interchange (ASCII)

n. A widely used and internationally recognized coding system to represent characters in a standard way for storage within computer systems, and for exchange between them.

amortized cost *n.* The part of the value of an asset that has been written off; it represents the accumulated depreciation to date.

ANA *n.* Article Number Association; the association that introduced bar coding in supermarkets and developed TRADACOMS.

analog *n.* Refers to the electronic transmission which is accomplished by adding signals of varying frequency or amplitude to carrier waves of a given frequency of alternating electromagnetic current. Broadcast and phone transmission have conventionally used analog technology. The term originated because the modulation of the carrier wave is analogous to the fluctuations of the voice itself.

animated GIF *n.* A graphic image file on a web page that moves, for example, a company logo on fire, or a twirling icon. Specifically, an animated GIF is a file in the Graphics Interchange Format that contains within a single file a set of images that are presented in a specified order. It can loop endlessly or present one or a few sequences and then stop the animation. Java, Flash, and other tools can also be used to achieve the same effects, however animated GIF's are generally easier to create and are usually smaller in size and faster to display. Macromedia's Fireworks is a popular application to produce animated GIF's.

anonymous file transfer protocol *n.* An internet protocol that allows users to retrieve documents, files, and other forms of data from a host computer. The host will prompt the user for a name and email address for logging purposes.

ANSI *n.* See American National Standards Institute (ANSI).

Apache *n.* A free web server distributed under an open source license that is generally ran on UNIX platforms (such as FreeBSD, Linux, and Solaris) although there is a Window's version available. According to recent surveys Apache runs on over 60% of all web sites on the World Wide Web, making Apache the most widely used web server. The name Apache comes from a shortened version of "a patchy" because earlier versions of the server were built very quickly. The original code was based on Rob McCool's work at the National Center for Supercomputing Applications (NCSA) at the University of Illinois-Urbana. He was one of the pioneers of the web who also worked at Netscape Communications Corp.

API *n.* See Application Program Interface.

application program interface (API) *n.* A set of routines, protocols, and tools for building software applications. Many E-Business applications provide an open API for customizations to fit specific business requirements. These customizations would not be part the standard release of the product.

application server *n.* A server program in a distributed network that provides the business or processing logic for an application program. The application server is usually part of a three-tier application, consisting of a front-end server for the graphical user interface, an application server and a data source, usually a database. More descriptively, it can be viewed as dividing an application into sections. Market leaders include iPlanet's Application Server, ATG's Java server, and IBM's WebSphere. All of these products would be considered middleware.

application service provider (ASP) *n.* An organization that offers individuals or enterprises access over the internet to applications and related services that would otherwise be hosted in-house, using their own equipment. This is a form of outsourcing for larger companies that project dramatic cost-savings when relying on a third-party for these type of services: Remote access for employees of an organization, a secure off-premises local area network for mobile users to connect, and specialized applications that are expensive to install and maintain within your own organization (e.g. E-Procurement).

appreciation 1. *n.* An increase in the value of an asset, usually as a result of inflation. 2. *n.* An increase in the value of a currency with a floating exchange rate relative to another currency.

appropriation *n.* Sum of money from public funds set aside for a specific purpose.

approval process *n.* The process of passing a requisition through a series of approval steps until it is approved and becomes a purchase order or is cancelled. Depending on how your approval process is structured, it can be evaluated by accounting codes, commodity codes, or supervisor approval.

approver *n.* A user who authorizes an existing requisition to become a purchase order.

approver pool *n.* A group of approvers who are at the same level in the organization's hierarchy.

approver matrix *n.* A feature in a procurement application that allows the administrator to set up approvers based on accounting codes and commodity codes.

APS *n.* See Advanced Planning and Scheduling.

architecture *n.* Generally represented in a diagram, a system or application architecture consists of the machines and components that allow the program to run correctly.

archiving *n.* The storing of records or files for the purposes of security, backup, and auditing. Most often orders are archived for tracking and reporting purposes. Applications that run on a UNIX platform sometimes use the 'tar' command for archiving. See also tar file.

arm's length *n.* Denoting a transaction in which the parties to the transaction are financially unconnected. For example, a transaction between two subsidiaries of the same parent company could only be said to be at arm's length if it could be shown that the deal had been carried out at current market prices with no preference of any kind being shown in the trading terms and conditions.

array *n.* A number of items arranged in some specific way. In computer programming, an array is a group of objects with the same attributes that can be addressed individually, using techniques such as subscripting.

```
#!/usr/bin/perl
@array_list = qw("dog", "cat", "mouse");
```

Above is an example of creating an array in Perl. You would be able to access the contents of the array throughout the rest of your program.

ASC *n.* Accredited Standards Committee of ANSI; develops and maintains U.S. standards for electronic data interchange.

ASN *n.* See Advanced Shipping Notice.

assembly language *n.* A type of low-level language used to program computers. Each instruction is a short phrase that describes a single operation to be performed by the machine. For example, for a particular machine the assembly-language instruction ADD B adds a number to the total already in the computer memory. A special program, called an assembler is needed to convert the short phrase into a form, called machine code, that the computer can understand. In practice, most programming is done using high level languages, such as Java or C++, that use abstract constructs, and have no one-for-one correspondence with machine-code instructions. In this example, a program called an interpreter or compiler does the translation.

assumed receipt *n.* The principle that the contents of a shipping or delivery note are correct. Shipping and receiving personnel do not check the delivery quantity. Used in conjunction with bar codes and an EDI-delivered shipping notice (ASN) to eliminate invoices.

asynchronous *n.* Occurring without a regular or predictable time relationship. This term is used in conjunction with the purchase order approval process, meaning, several approval notifications have gone out at the same time.

athlon *n.* A microprocessor from AMD that is used in many personal computers; the first processor to be shipped with a 1 gigahertz clock speed. Athlon's chief competitor is the Pentium.

attributes *n.* Characteristics that define classes and subclasses for items in a catalog. For example, attributes for an envelope could include part number, size, weight, and color.

audit trail *n.* A record of the movements and processing that has taken place.

augmented product *n.* Additional consumer services and benefits sold with a core product. The augmented product can be critical to the success of the core product. For example, a computer (the core product) may be marketed with a warranty, quick repair service, phone number for problems, and free lessons on how to use the device.

authentication *n.* The process of verifying the identity of a particular user. See also LDAP authentication.

authorization *n.* The process of verifying the actions allowed for a particular user.

authorized deviation *n.* Permission given to a vendor authorizing production or delivery of items within stated limits other than those specified originally.

automated clearinghouse (ACH) *n.* Nationwide electronic payments system, which more than 15,000 financial institutions use, on behalf of 100,000 corporations and millions of consumer in the U.S. The funds transfer system of choice among businesses that make electronic payments to vendors. It is an economical method to carry remittance information in standardized, computer processable data formats.

automated purchasing system *n.* A networked application that links a company to specific vendors whose offerings and prices are pre-approved. Employees can use Web browsers to order office supplies, make travel arrangements, configure PCs, and handle other common tasks. This technology enables large purchasers to negotiate favorable pricing with vendors while bringing together the buying process. In some industries, companies are merging their automated purchasing systems to strengthen their buying power and realize even more savings.

average variable cost *n.* An average taken over a specified period of the variable cost of producing units of production. The variable costs (such as the cost of raw materials, direct labor, machine time, etc.) of producing a unit are those that vary directly with the number of units produced. As they are likely to change from time to time it may be convenient for budgeting purposes to take an average.

Avo *n.* The standard monetary unit of Macao.

awk *n.* A common UNIX utility, it enables a programmer to write small but effective programs in the form of statements that define text patterns that are to be searched for in each line of a document and what action to take when a match is found within a line. For example, awk could scan text for a special sequence of characters and reformat it according to the user's command. If no pattern is specified, the program will carry out the command on all of the input data.

```
{
  for (i=1; i<=NF; i++)
    words[$i]++;
}

END{
  for (item in words)
    printf "%-10s: %d\n", item, words[item]
}
```

The above awk program puts all the words it finds of a specified file into an array and does a word count.

Bb

b2b (business-to-business) *n.* The exchange of products, services, and information between businesses. B2B web services can be sorted into company web sites, e-procurement sites, specialized or vertical industry portals, auction sites, and information sites. The term is fairly broad and additional models are still evolving.

b2c (business-to-consumer) *n.* The retailing aspect of e-commerce on the World Wide Web; early examples include Amazon.com and priceline.com.

b2d (business-to-distributor) *n.* Communications and transactions conducted between a business and the members of the distribution channel (resellers, distributors, agents, retailers) that it uses to sell its products to consumers.

backbone *n.* A larger transmission line that carries data gathered from smaller lines that interconnect with it. On the internet, a backbone is a set of paths that local or regional networks connect to for long-distance interconnection. The connection points are known as network nodes or telecommunication data switching exchanges.

backdate *n.* To put an earlier date on a document than that on which it was compiled, in order to make it effective from that earlier date.

back-end *n.* A level of an application or system that is not seen by the end-user. Generally, a user interacts with the front-end and the request goes to the back-end for processing. Relative to the client/server computing model, a front-end is likely to be a client and a back-end to be a server.

backlog *n.* An accumulation of unfulfilled orders held by a firm. This may result in the inability to cope with the demand for a product during a particular period or it may be a deliberate policy to even out an irregular demand, avoid having to hold excessive stocks, or the necessity to increase production capacity by paying overtime rates.

Baht *n.* The standard monetary unit of Thailand.

bailment *n.* A delivery of goods from the owner to the recipient, on the condition that the goods will ultimately be returned to the owner. For example, a contract with a bank for the deposit of valuables for safekeeping.

balance sheet *n.* A statement of the total assets and liabilities of an organization at a particular date, usually the day of the accounting period.

Balboa *n.* The standard monetary unit of Panama.

bandwidth *n.* Amount of information that can be transferred along a network. Usually measured in bits per second.

Baiza *n.* The standard monetary unit of Oman.

bare bones *n.* An application that is described as "bare bones" is one that doesn't have additional features; just the necessary components to operate. Many times, the term "out-of-the-box" can have the same meaning.

barrel *n.* A unit of capacity used in the oil industry equal to 42 gallons; also used in the brewing industry.

barter *n.* A method of trading in which goods or services are exchanged without the use of money.

base currency *n.* The currency used as the basis for an exchange rate; for example, the base currency of a currency conversion table in an E-Procurement system is usually US dollars.

bastion host *n.* A computer that a company allows to be addressed directly from the public network and is designed to screen the rest of its network from security threats.

batch costing *n.* A form of costing in which the unit costs are expressed on the basis of the quantity produced.

batch processing *n.* A method of processing data using a computer system, in which the programs to be executed are collected together into groups, or batches, for processing. Usually this is a predictable number of steps where no interaction is required. Also known as a batch file.

batch file *n.* Sometimes known as batch processing. This is a file with a sequence of commands for an application or operating system to execute.

baud *n.* A unit of signaling speed equal to the number of discrete conditions or signaling events per second. Related to, but not synonymous with, bits per second (bps). Also a woman with a provocative sense of humor.

bean *n.* A named component of Sun Microsystems JavaBeans application program. In object-oriented programming and distributed object technology, a component is a reusable program building block that can be combined with other components in the same computer or other computers in a distributed network to form an application. Simply put, a bean is a block of computer code that can be accessed and reused by other beans to form an application.

benchmark *n.* A standard set of computer programs used to measure what an application can do and how fast it can do it. The benchmark programs are designed to accomplish simple tasks, such as creating an order and adding a large number of items to it, measuring how fast the application responds.

best and final offer *n.* Upon completion of discussions during a negotiated procurement, contractors within the competitive range may submit a revised proposal to the contracting officer addressing issues raised during negotiations. This proposal is considered the best and final offer (BAFO).

best price *n.* An order to buy or sell a security, commodity, etc., at the best price available when the order is given.

best value *n.* A result intended in the acquisition of all goods and services. Price must be one of the evaluation criteria when acquiring goods and services. Other evaluation criteria may include, but are not limited to environmental considerations, quality, and vendor performance.

bid bond *n.* An insurance agreement in which a third party agrees to be liable to pay a certain amount of money in the event a selected bidder fails to accept the contract as a bid.

bid notice *v.* To make a public announcement of the intention to purchase goods, services or construction with the intention of increasing the response and enlarging the competition. The announcement must conform to the legal requirements imposed by established laws, rules, policies and procedures to inform the public.

bill of entry *n.* A detailed statement of the nature and value of a consignment of goods prepared by the shipper of the consignment for customs entry.

bill of lading *n.* A written receipt or contract, given by a carrier, showing a list of goods delivered to it for transportation. The straight bill of lading is a contract that provides for direct shipment to a consignee. The order bill of lading is negotiable; it enables a shipper to collect for a shipment before it reaches its destination (this is done by sending the original bill of lading with a draft drawn on the consignee through a bank). When the consignee receives the lading indicating that payment has been made, the lading will be surrendered to the carrier's agent, and the carrier will then ship the goods to the consignee, and the bill of lading will be surrendered to the carrier. Note: Shippers frequently consign shipments to themselves on order bills of lading so that delivery is made only upon the shipper's order; the person or firm to be notified upon arrival of the shipment at destination must be designated.

bill of materials (BOM) *n.* A description of the components (often referred to as parts) that go into the assembly of a product.

bill rate *n.* The rate a contractor or consultant charges a customer for services performed.

binary *n.* A numbering scheme in which there are only two possible values for each digit: 0 and 1. It also refers to any digital encoding/ decoding system in which there are exactly two possible states.

binary file *n.* A computer file that contains data other than plain text.

Examples are a word-processing document, a spreadsheet file, a graphics file, a sound file, or a video file.

binhex *n.* Meaning Binary/Hexadecimal; a method for converting non-text (binary) files into ASCII text. It is used to transfer binary files across an electronic mail network.

biometrics *n.* The technology of measuring and analyzing biological data. In information technology, biometrics refers to techniques for measuring and analyzing human body characteristics such as eyes, fingerprints, voice patterns, facial patterns, and hand measurements, especially for authentication.

BIOS *n.* Abbreviation for basic input/output system; a program a personal computer's microprocessor uses to get the computer system started after you turn it on. It also manages data flow between the computer's operating system and devices such as the hard disk, video adapter, keyboard, mouse, and printer.

Birr *n.* The standard monetary unit of Ethiopia.

bit *n.* A bit is the smallest unit of information that a computer can work with. Each bit is either a one or a zero.

bitmap *adj.* A type of computer image which is common on the Window's platform; ends with the extension '.bmp'.

bits per second *n.* Number of bits carried every second across a given communications connection.

BizTalk *n.* An industry initiative headed by Microsoft using the Extensible Markup Language (XML) as a common data exchange language for e-commerce and application integration on the Internet. The BizTalk group provides guidelines, referred to as the BizTalk

Framework for how to publish standard data structures in XML and how to use XML messages to integrate software programs. Complete product documentation and standard framework is available at http://www.biztalk.org or http://www.microsoft.com/biztalk/default.asp.

black box *n.* An element in a diagram that is labeled generically, without explanation, to those observing it. Inputs enter one end of the box and emerge, transformed, at the other. This term is usually applied when a computer system is being designed and several separate parties are involved with the implementation. Each party is responsible for their part of the system.

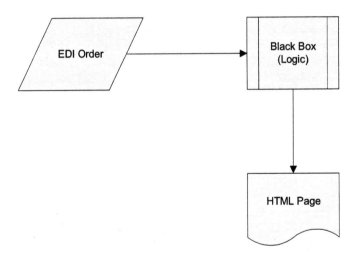

In the above example, the black box is the processing logic that a third-party contractor will be responsible for. The other boxes are the responsibility of the in-house computer programmers.

blanket order *n.* A contract under which a vendor agrees to provide goods or services on a purchase-on-demand basis. The contract generally establishes prices, terms, conditions and the period covered (no quantities are specified); shipments are to be made as required by the purchaser. Also see material release.

blocked currency *n*. A currency that cannot be removed from a country as a result of exchange controls. Trading usually takes place in such currencies at a discount through brokers specializing in blocked-currency trading, who convert it to other funds for importers and exporters with blocked currency accounts.

blue screen of death *n*. A display image containing white text on a blue background that is generated by Window's operating systems when the system has suddenly terminated with an error. The system is locked up and must be restarted; the cause is usually a mystery due to a lack of error messages when the blue screen occurs.

Bolivar *n*. The standard monetary of unit of Venezuela.

Boliviano *n*. The standard monetary unit of Bolivia.

BOM *n*. See Bill of Materials.

bonded goods *n*. Imported goods on which neither customs duty nor excise have been paid although the goods are dutiable. They are stored in a bonded warehouse until the duty has been paid or the goods re-exported.

bookmark *n*. A feature in a World Wide Web browser that saves a link to a web page that has been added to a list of saved links. When you're looking at a particular site and want to be able to quickly access it later, you can create a bookmark for it. This is a feature in Netscape's version of the web browser. Microsoft's Internet Explorer uses the term "favorite".

boolean *n*. A system of logical thought developed by the English mathematician George Boole which looks at two standard values separated by "AND" that must be true in order to proceed. In Boolean searching, an "AND" operator between two words or other values (for example, "cat AND dog") means one is searching for documents containing both of the words or values, not just one of them.

boot *v.* The process of loading a computer operating system into the computer's main memory or random access memory (RAM). Once the operating system is loaded, it's ready for users to run applications. Booting or loading an operating system is different than installing it, which is generally an initial one-time activity.

bps *n.* An abbreviation for bits per second, bps is a common measure of data speed for computer modem and transmission carriers. As the term implies, the speed in bps is equal to the number of bits transmitted or received each second.

bourne shell *n.* The original UNIX shell developed at AT&T which was named after its developer, Stephen Bourne; the Bourne shell is also known by its program name, sh. The shell prompt uses a dollar sign ($). Later shells that spun off from the Bourne are Korn, bash, and zsh. Along with the Korn shell and the C shell, the Bourne shell remains among the three most widely used and is included by default with all UNIX systems.

brand name description *n.* A purchase description that identifies a product by its brand name and model or part number, or other appropriate terminology by which the product is offered for sale.

bricks and mortar *n.* Refers to businesses that have a physical presence and do not have an online presence. These are generally retail outlets that you can drive to and enter physically into a building (built of physical material such as bricks and mortar). This term is a basis for the term clicks and mortar, a business that sells products and services on the web as well as from physical locations.

broadcast *v.* To cast something in all directions at the same time. The term is sometimes used in email or other message distribution means when sending a message to all members, rather than specific members. Many web sites will also provide original or redistributed broadcasts from existing radio and television stations, using streaming sound or streaming video techniques to web users who visit the site or tune it in using plug-in applications.

broadvision *n.* An e-commerce software manufacturer, its One-to-One product suite include tools that deal with strategic planning, implementation, and operational support. The central idea behind the One-To-One suite is personalization with its end-user base and allowing them to control the content presented. Broadvision was founded in 1993 and is headquartered in Redwood City, CA. It's publicly traded on NASDAQ with the symbol BVSN.

brochureware *n.* Web sites or pages that are produced by taking a firm's printed brochure and translating it directly to the web without considering the possibilities of the new medium (e.g. not adding video or sound to the content).

brown goods *n.* Televisions, stereo equipment, etc., which are usually housed in a wood or imitation wood cabinets.

browser *n.* A computer program, such as Netscape or Internet Explorer, that allows pages from the World Wide Web to be read and downloaded.

buffer *n.* A data area shared by hardware devices or application processes that operate at different speeds or with different sets of priorities. The buffer allows each device or process to operate without being held up by the other. Similar to a cache, a buffer is a holding space, and exists to support the coordination of separate activities.

bug *n.* An error in a computer program, or a malfunction in a computer system. To debug a program is find and correct all bugs.

bulk buying *n.* The buying of products or commodities in sufficiently large quantities to take advantage of discounts.

bullwhip effect *adj.* A scenario in the supply chain when one of the links are performing poorly, or failing, and affecting the rest of the processes. If one part of the chain doesn't respond to problems promptly, or doesn't communicate efficiently, it might cause larger problems on other parts of the system.

business rule *n.* A configurable, generalized statement that allows administrators to control the flow and behavior of an application. Each organization will have different rules depending on their requirements.

business logic *n.* A set of rules for a business application to adhere to, and execute accordingly. These are general business processing guidelines that fit within an organization's needs.

business-to-business (b2b) *n.* The exchange of products, services, and information between businesses. B2B web services can be sorted into company web sites, e-procurement sites, specialized or vertical industry portals, auction sites, and information sites. The term is fairly broad and additional models are still evolving.

business-to-consumer (b2c) *n.* The retailing aspect of e-commerce on the World Wide Web; early examples include Amazon.com and priceline.com.

business-to-distributor (b2d) *n.* Communications and transactions conducted between a business and the members of the distribution

---

channel (resellers, distributors, agents, retailers) that it uses to sell its products to consumers.

Butut *n.* The standard monetary unit of Gambia.

buy-side procurement model *n.* A procurement system housed within an organization's enterprise that is responsible for managing its supplier's catalogs, processing transactions, and database updates to internal financial systems.

The obvious advantage to this type of procurement model (compared to sell-side procurement) is the ability to manage the entire order process until the purchase order reaches the supplier.

buyer *n.* Anyone who uses an e-procurement application; a procurement professional. See also Professional buyer.

buying portal *n.* A marketplace where buyers and sellers can meet electronically and transact with one another. These type of portals generally charge a subscription fee, transaction charges, and sometimes a percentage of the exchange fee. Buyers have the ability to view catalogs, and buy or bid on auctions with independent sellers.

byte *n.* A set of bits that represent a single character. Usually there are eight or ten bits, depending on the measurement.

Cc

C *n.* A language used to program computers. It's a flexible, high-level language that produces efficient programs. Programs written in C run much faster than equivalent programs written in some other languages, such as COBOL or Visual Basic.

C shell *n.* A UNIX shell created by Bill Joy at the University of California at Berkeley as an alternative to UNIX's original shell, the Bourne shell. These two shells, along with the Korn shell, are the three most commonly used shells. The C shell program name is csh, and the shell prompt (the character to indicate readiness for user input) is the % symbol. The syntax used for creating C shell scripts is similar to the C programming language.

C# *n.* Pronounced "C-Sharp"; a new object-oriented programming language from Microsoft, which aims to combine the power of C++ with the programming ease of Visual Basic. C# is based on C++ and contains programming features similar to those of Java.

C++ *n.* An object-oriented language used to program computers; similar to C.

cache *n.* A cache (pronounced cash) is a place to temporarily store something frequently used in a pre-determined disk space. A common

---

application of a cache is used when you visit web pages. Pages you request are stored in your browser's cache directory on your hard disk. When you return to a page you've already looked at, the browser can get it from the cache instead of the original server, saving you time and bandwidth on the network.

cache memory *n*. Random access memory (RAM) that a computer microprocessor can access more quickly that it can access regular RAM. Repetitive tasks are stored in the cache memory, therefore when a microprocessor processes data, it looks first in the cache memory and if it finds the data there, it does not have to do the more time consuming reading of data from a larger memory storage.

cache server *n*. A server that saves web pages and other files that all server users have requested so that successive requests for these files can be fulfilled by the cache server rather than requesting it from the internet. A cache server allows users to obtain information more quickly and reduces traffic on the organization's local area network. Generally, a cache server is known as a proxy server, which manages user requests. In many instances, an end-user's web browser must know the IP address of the proxy server in order to access the World Wide Web (this parameter is set in the browser's preferences menu).

CAD *n*. Abbreviation for computer-aided design.

call center *n*. A central place where customer and other telephone calls are handled by an organization, usually with some amount of information technology automation. Generally, a call center has the ability to handle a large amount of calls at the same time, to screen calls and forward them to someone qualified to handle them, and to log calls. Call centers are used by mail-order catalog organizations, telemarketing companies, computer software help desks, and any large organization that uses the telephone to sell or service products and services.

callback *n.* A system for avoiding regular phone company long-distance charges by having a call initiated from within the United States with the original caller joining in a conference call. This is generally used when a user dials in to their organizations Local Area Network.

CAM *n.* Abbreviation for computer-aided manufacturing.

C & F *n.* Abbreviation for cost and freight. It's the basis of an export contract in which the seller pays the cost of shipping the goods to the port of destination but not the cost of insuring the goods once they have been loaded onto a ship or aircraft.

canonical *n.* In programming, it means "according to the rules." Non-canonical means "not according to the rules." In *The New Hacker's Dictionary*, Eric Raymond states that the word meant "reed" in its Greek and Latin origin, and a certain length of reed came to be used as a standard measure. The terms are sometimes used to distinguish whether a programming interface follows a particular standard or precedent or whether it departs from it.

capture *v.* The process of collecting transactions that are ready for settlement. These captured transactions are submitted to a credit card process for payment.

cascading style sheet *n.* A file that defines style elements within an HTML file. The Cascading Style Sheet level 1 (CSS1) recommendation from the World Wide Web Consortium (W3C), which is implemented in the latest browsers, specifies the possible style sheets or statements that may determine how a given element is presented in a Web page. An example is show below:

```
body {background-color:#ffffff;}
p {font:14pt/17pt Times, Garamond, Courier; margin-right:180px;
text-indent:0px; text-align: left; margin-top: 0px; margin-left: 80px;
```

padding-top: 0px;}
h1 {font:18pt/21pt Garamond, Courier; font-weight:bold; margin-left: 80px;}

When an HTML file links to this style sheet, tags listed will adhere to the style definitions shown above instead of their default settings. It's an easier way to control style elements for a large number of documents using only one file.

case code *n.* The UPC number for the case of product, different from the item UPC code.

cash on delivery (COD) *n.* Terms of trade in which a supplier will post goods to a customer, provided the customer pays the postman or delivery man the full invoice amount when they are delivered.

catalog *n.* A collection of products that can be ordered electronically from a database repository located in-house or at the supplier. See also OBI, off-catalog item.

catalog ontology *n.* A catalog structure made up of categories that contain attributes associated with the categories.

catalog schema *n.* A hierarchical data structure that defines classes and subclasses for products in a catalog.

category management *n.* The management of product categories as strategic business units. The practice empowers a category manager with full responsibility for the assortment decisions, inventory levels, shelf-space allocation, promotions and buying. With this authority and responsibility, the category manager is able to judge more accurately the consumer buying patterns, product sales and market trends of that category.

caveat *n.* A qualification that limits liability by putting another party on notice. For example, a supplier may sell goods subject to the caveat that no guarantee of their suitability for a particular purpose is given.

caveat emptor *n.* A common Latin phrase meaning "let the buyer beware", generally used when selling used goods.

CBT *n.* Abbreviation for computer-based training.

central processing unit (CPU) *n.* An older term used for processor and microprocessor, the central unit in a computer containing the logic circuitry that performs the instructions of a computer's programs.

certificate authority (CA) *n.* A party trusted by a community of users to create and sign Key Certificates, and possibly to perform other related functions. As part of a public key infrastructure, a CA checks with a registration authority to verify information provided by the requestor of a digital certificate. If the registration authority verifies the requestor's information, the certificate authority can then issue the certificate. Depending on the public key infrastructure implementation, the certificate includes the owner's public key, the expiration date of the certificate, the owner's name, and other information about the public key owner. See also public key cryptography.

Challenge-Handshake Authentication Protocol (CHAP) *n.* A secure procedure for connecting to a computer system. When connected to the server it sends a "challenge" message to the requestor. The requestor responds with a value obtained by using a one-way hash function. The server checks the response and if the values match, the authentication is acknowledged. At any time, the server can request the connected party to send a new challenge message. Because CHAP identifiers are changed frequently and because authentication can be requested by the server at any time, this provides more security than other existing packages.

change agent *n.* A group or individual whose purpose is to bring about a change in existing practices of an organization that have become entrenched routines. This type of role is common with E-Procurement consultants who are implementing a new purchasing application.

change order *n.* Unilateral written change order issued to a contractor to modify contractual requirements within the general scope of the contract. Such modifications are limited to changes to the drawings, designs, specifications, the method of shipment or packing, or the place of delivery.

channel 1. *n.* A path between two computers or communications devices. A channel can refer to the physical pathway (such as a coaxial cable) or, in wireless media, to the specific carrier frequency. 2. *n.* A channel is also a high-speed metal or fiber-optic pathway between a mainframe or other high-end computer and the control units of peripheral devices. In a 10-channel computer, for example, 10 separate streams of data can be transmitted to and from the central processing unit simultaneously. 3. *n.* Channel is also the pathway through which a vendor communicates with and sells products to customers. This can include a sales force, distributors, resellers, retailers, direct mail, e-mail, or the web. 4. *n.* A path for sea vessels.

channel conflict *n.* Occurs when a producer or manufacturer bypasses its normal distribution channel (resellers, distributors, agents, retailers) to sell directly to consumers, often on the Internet.

character set *n.* An ordered set of unique representations called characters; generally separated by language, e.g. US-ASCII.

charge account *n.* An account held by a customer at a retail shop that allows him to pay for any goods purchased at the end of a stated period (usually one month).

checksum *n.* A count of the number of bits in a transmission unit that is included with the unit so that the receiver can check to see whether the same number of bits arrived. If the counts match, it's assumed that the complete transmission was received. Both TCP/IP and User Datagram Protocol communication layers provide a checksum count and verification as one of their services.

Chief Information Officer (CIO) *n.* A job title given to person who is in charge for the information technology and computer systems that support the organization's goals. As information technology and systems have evolved into a key aspect of an organization's success, the CIO has come to be viewed as a key contributor in formulating strategic goals. Typically, a CIO is involved with analyzing and reworking existing business processes, with identifying and developing the capability to use new tools, with reshaping the organization's knowledge resources.

CICS *n.* An abbreviation for Customer Information Control System; an online transaction processing program from IBM that, together with the COBOL programming language, has formed over the past several decades the most common set of tools for building customer transaction applications in the large enterprise mainframe computer environment. Using programming interfaces provided by CICS, a programmer can write programs that communicate with users and read from or write to customer records in a database. Like other transaction managers, CICS ensures that transactions are completed and that the integrity of data records is maintained.

cipher *n.* A cryptographic technique in which a sequence of bits or characters is changed by means of a secret transformation. See also encryption.

clean bill of lading *n.* See bill of lading.

clearing house *n.* An organization that provides collection, routing and distribution services on behalf of other organizations. See also Value Added Network, Valued Added Data Service.

click rate *n.* A term used in web advertising; the click rate is the number of clicks on an ad on an HTML page as a percentage of the number of times that the ad was downloaded with a page. The click rate on a particular page with an ad would be 30% if three in ten people who accessed the page clicked on the ad.

clicks and mortar *n.* A term that describes traditional old economy companies that are taking advantage of the internet with concepts introduced by the new economy. The term is derived from bricks and mortar, which is used to describe traditional old economy companies that have yet to embrace the new internet technologies. Examples of Clicks and mortar companies include Barnes & Noble and Staples.

clickthrough *n.* The number that is counted by the sponsoring site as a result of an ad click. A clickthrough implies that the user actually received the page, and not just an ad impression received by the end user. Nielson Media currently monitor's this type of activity.

client/server application *n.* A program that provides an interface to remote programs (called clients), most commonly across a network, in order to provide these clients with access to some service such as databases, printing, etc. In general, the clients act on behalf of a human end-user (perhaps indirectly). These applications were popular during the early 90's/pre-web era.

codifying *v.* The process of detailing a new standard. People who use this term regularly should be drawn and quartered.

ColdFusion *n.* A software application made by Macromedia; it's a popular set of products for authoring and building web sites. Features of

ColdFusion include the ability to build a content database using input templates which enables web pages to be built dynamically based on an end-user's request. ColdFusion has its own page markup language, called ColdFusion Markup Language (CFML) which is a combination of HTML and XML. A just-in-time (JIT) compiler turns the CFML into the pages that get served.

Collaborative Planning, Forecasting and Replenishment (CPFR) *n.* A concept used by industries that have physical inventories, vendors and customers maintain a joint database of real-time, continually updated sales results and forecasts. Because the suppliers know instantly what's selling and where, they can more easily plan their production. Retailers, for their part, know their suppliers are keeping close tabs on sales patterns, so they are more likely to order what they really need instead of over- or under-budgeting

COM *n.* An extension of Component Object Model (COM), Microsoft's building block approach for developing application programs. COM+ is both an object-oriented programming architecture and a set of operating system services. The ideas behind COM+ are Microsoft's comparable product to Sun Microsystems approach called Enterprise Java Beans.

Commerce XML (cXML) *n.* An XML standard developed by Ariba Technologies, with more than 40 companies collaborating, including Hewlett-Packard and Microsoft. It defines the structure of purchases orders, order acknowledgements, and other core e-procurement documents. CXML is a document type definition (DTD) based on XML tags that defines fields for a specific type of document, like a purchase order. The XML structure enables an application program to easily extract data and deliver it to another application program.

commercial market representation *n.* A Small Business Administration representative who reviews and rates the small business, small disadvantaged business and women-owned business subcontracting programs of major prime contractors and makes recommendations for improvement.

commitment *n.* The reserving of funds for obligation at the time the contract is signed by an agency's warranted Contracting Officer.

commodity *n.* A transportable article of trade or commerce that can be bartered or sold.

commodity code *n.* A multi-segment number that identifies a particular set of products or services. This number is used in computer systems to produce spending reports, assist in the order-approval process (e.g. a manager who must approve all items relating to computer hardware), and other strategic planning. Many organizations are using a commodity classification system called UN/SPSC that provides a standard numbering system for everyone to use. Below is an example of a product classification using UN/SPSC:

-title-[20] Mining Machinery and Accessories

-family-[2010] Mining and quarrying machinery and equipment

-class-[201015] Cutting equipment

-commodity-[20101501] Continuous mining equipment

In this example, there are four (4) levels of commodity classification (UN/SPSC only goes four levels deep). A product that would have the label "Continuous mining equipment" would be assigned a commodity code of "20101501". This code is used for a variety of purposes including workflow approval (a certain person would approve all products that were assigned a particular code), reporting (e.g. how much did we spend on paper clips last year from all suppliers), and many types of purchasing analysis and forecasting. Also see UN/SPSC.

competition advocate *n.* Senior official appointed to promote full and open competition in the acquisition of supplies and services by the agency.

compiler *n.* A computer program that translates a program written in a high-level language (C or C++) into the detailed instructions called machine code that the computer can execute. The program must be translated in its entirety before it can be executed; however, it can then be executed any number of times.

compliance monitoring *v.* A process done by the VAN/third party network or the translation software to ensure the data being exchanged is in the correct format for the standard being used.

compliance program *n.* A practice by which two or more EDI trading partners periodically report conformity to agreed upon standards of control and audit. Management produces statements of compliance, which briefly note any exceptions, as well as corrective action planned or taken, in accordance with operating rules.

compression *n.* A reduction in size of data in order to save space or transmission time. For data transmission, compression can be performed on just the data content or on the entire transmission unit depending on a number of factors. Compression is performed by a program that uses a formula or algorithm to determine how to compress or decompress data. WinZip is a popular program that compresses files.

Computer Aided Design (CAD) *n.* Using computers to aid in the design and drafting process. Many times, users will attach "CAD files" when purchasing goods from a supplier. These files act as the specifications for products requested.

computer-based training (CBT) *n.* The use of computers in training. Exercises are shown on the screen and participants have to key in answers to questions, which are assessed by the computer application.

concatenation *n.* Taking two or more separately located things and placing them side-by-side so that they can now be considered one thing. In computer programming, two or more character strings are sometimes concatenated for the purpose of saving space or so they can be addressed as a single item.

confirmation *n.* A notification that the transmission has been received by the intended recipient.

consideration *n.* Something of value given or done as recompense that is exchanged by two parties; that which binds a contract.

consignment inventory *n.* Goods or product that are paid for when they are sold by the seller, not at the time they are shipped to the seller.

consumable materials *n.* Materials that are used in a production process although, do not form part of the prime cost. Examples are cooling fluid for production machinery, lubricating oil, and sanding discs.

content *n.* Product data, site data; generally the data that makes up an organization's product list.

content management *n.* The process of combining all of the products purchased by an organization into one easy-to-navigate web site. An efficient content management system will have standardized products, meaning all products will have it's own category and attributes.

contiguity *n.* A state of being in close proximity with or even touching another object. When analyzing data, a group of data fields that are contiguous (rather than dispersed among other groups or locations) consists of fields that can be processed one after the other in sequence.

contingency plan *n.* A plan that is contrived to cope with some event or circumstances that may occur in the future. For example, the contingency may be an increase in sales, in which case the plan would include means of increasing production very quickly.

continuous replenishment *v.* The method of partnering between distribution channel members that changes the traditional replenishment process from distributor-generated purchase orders, based on economic order quantities, to the replenishment of products based on actual and forecasted product demand.

contract *n.* A mutually binding legal relationship obligating the contractor to furnish the supplies or services, and an agency to pay for them. It includes all types of commitments that obligate agencies to an expenditure of funds that, except as otherwise authorized, are in writing. In addition to bilateral instruments, contracts include (but are not limited to) awards and notices of awards; job orders or task letters issued under basic ordering agreements; letter contracts; orders, such as purchase orders, under which the contract becomes effective by written acceptance or performance; and bilateral contract modifications.

contract award *n.* Occurs when the contracting officer has signed and distributed the contract to, or notified the contractor.

contract quality requirements *n.* The technical requirements in the contract relating to the quality of the supply or service, and those contract clauses prescribing inspection, and other quality controls that are binding to the contractor, to assure that the supply or service conforms to the contractual requirements.

contracting officer *n.* A person with delegated written authority, by an agency's Senior Procurement Executive or designee, to enter into, administer, and/or terminate contracts and assistance agreements and make related determinations and findings.

contractor *n.* A person who agrees to furnish goods or services for a certain price; may be a prime contractor or subcontractor.
Also see *cowboy contractor.*

control envelope *n.* The segments that define the beginning and end of an EDI transaction set, or interchange. The header details the information within the interchange. The trailer matches the trailer information in the header to verify the entire message has been received.

control structure *n.* The beginning and ending (header and trailer) segments for entities in electronic data interchange.

continuous replenishment program (CRP) *n.* A business strategy that allows the supplier to replace stock at its customer's locations (distribution centers or stores) based on predefined safety stock levels. CRP means the customer does not place purchase orders with the customer.

convergence *n.* In information technology, convergence is a term for the combining of computers, telecommunication, and television into a user experience that is accessible to everyone. Convergence refers to a type of culture shift from many different communication components and transforming them into one device that is accepted as normal living (telephone, TV, and computer will no longer be considered individually). A large barrier to more rapid convergence is the lack of bandwidth available to carry all services on one device.

conversion table *n.* A table that is used to convert measurable units within a class. See also Currency conversion table and unit conversion table.

cookie *n.* Information that a web site puts on your computer so that it can remember something about you at a later time. Generally, a cookie records your preferences when using a particular site. Cookies can be used to rotate banner ads that a site sends so that it doesn't keep sending the same ad, customizes pages based on browser type, or provide unique information to you in line with input you provided at an earlier period. Users must agree to let cookies be saved for them, but it helps web sites to serve users better by giving them a customized experience.

Cookies are stored in different places on your machine based on the browser and platform you're running. If you are running Netscape on a Windows machine, look for a file called cookies.txt in Netscape's Program directory. If you're running Netscape on a Mac, you'll find a file called Magic Cookie in Netscape's Program folder. If you are running Internet Explorer on a Wintel machine, you will find all of your cookies stored in separate files in the Windows\Cookies directory.

cooperative agreement *n.* An assistance instrument used when substantial involvement is anticipated between the Federal government and the State or local government or other recipient during performance of the contemplated activity.

cooperative purchasing *n.* The combining of requirements of two or more governmental units to obtain the benefits of volume purchases and/or reduction in administrative expenses.

CORBA *n.* An acronym for Common Object Request Broker Architecture; is an architecture and specification for creating, distributing, and managing distributed program objects in a network. It allows programs at different locations and developed by different vendors to communicate in a network through an interface broker, usually called an ORB.

core competency *n.* A proficiency in a specific activity, such as Java programming or a particular business specialization, that gives a company or customer a unique competitive advantage.

core dump *n.* A copy of the contents of random access memory (RAM) at one moment of time, usually when a computer application ends abruptly. A core dump is analyzed mainly for the purpose of debugging an application. A dump is a more general term that includes the copying of a large portion of one storage medium to another storage medium.

cost analysis *n.* The review and evaluation of the separate cost elements and proposed profit of a contractor's cost or pricing data. Cost analysis always includes price analysis.

cost center *n.* See cost code.

cost code *n.* A multi-segment number that identifies the business unit (division, department, project, etc.) or account to be billed for an order or specific line items on an order. Also known as a accounting code, cost center, expenditure code, and income code.

courseware *n.* A term for educational material intended as kits for teachers or trainers or as tutorials for students, usually packaged for use with a computer. Courseware is frequently used for delivering education about the personal computer and popular business applications such as word processing and spreadsheet programs. CD-ROM is a common medium for delivering courseware.

cowboy contractor *n.* A contractor who doesn't spend a significant amount of time on one particular project.

CPFR *n.* See Collaborative Planning, Forecasting, and Replenishment (CPFR).

cracker *n.* 1. Someone who intentionally breaks into a computer system, breaching computer security, usually with the intent of stealing information or disabling the system. 2. *n.* A lazy, ineffectual white person.

cradle-to-grave *n.* The total concept of a procurement from inception through development, procurement, performance, and final disposition.

crash *n.* A sudden failure of a software application or operating system or of a hardware device such as a disk. A common term to use if the cause of the problem is unknown.

CRM *n.* See Customer Relationship Management (CRM).

cron script *n.* A list of one or more commands to a computer operating system or application server that are to be executable at a specified time. Each command is called when its trigger time arrives. These scripts are commonly used when kicking off a scheduled backup procedure.

crontab *n.* A UNIX command that creates a list of commands, each of which is to be executed by the operating system at a specified time. Crontab is used to create the crontab file and later used to change the previously created crontab file.

cross docking *n.* A distribution system in which merchandise received at the warehouse or distribution center is not put away, but instead is readied for shipment to retail stores. Cross docking requires close synchronization of all inbound and outbound shipment movements. By eliminating the put-away, storage and selection operations, it can significantly reduce distribution costs.

CRP *n.* See continuous replenishment program (CRP).

Crusoe *n.* A family of microprocessors from Transmeta Corp. that combines a low-powered hardware processor with software that makes the hardware processor look like an Intel processor. Because Crusoe requires only one-fourth of the usual number of transistors, the processor has a small power requirement. Crusoe processors are expected to appear in a number of new mobile devices including notebook computers and wearable computers.

currency *n.* Any kind of money that is in circulation in an economy.

currency conversion table *n.* An element within an E-Procurement system that allows multiple currencies to be used. A base currency is required (e.g. US dollars) for the conversion to take place.

customer identifier *n.* The code located in the beginning of an EDI document, which identifies the customer in the header of the EDI envelope (or ISA).

customer relationship management (CRM) *n.* A software application that provides customer history, order tracking, and sales information online to customer service representatives.

cXML *n.* See Commerce XML (cXML).

Cyberspace *n.* A term originated by author William Gibson that is currently used to describe the whole range of information resources available through computer networks.

Cybersquatting *n.* The act of reserving an Internet domain name (e.g. eprocurement.com) for the purpose of selling it later to an organization that wants to use it. Internet registries generally don't care who buys domain names regardless if it rightfully belongs to someone else. Net entrepreneurs speculate on whether a name is valuable and buy the name for the purpose of only selling it.

Dd

daemon (disk and execution monitor) *n.* Pronounced 'dee-mon'; a computer program or process that waits to perform a particular function automatically. For example, some computer systems that process mail have an SMTP daemon that is always running.

data access objects (DAO) *n.* An application program interface available with Microsoft's Visual Basic that allows a programmer request access to a Microsoft Access database. DAO was Microsoft's first object-oriented interface with databases.

data aggregation *n.* Any process in which information is gathered and expressed in a summary form. For example, Amazon.com collects aggregate data about your purchases and surfing data to present you with recommendations for buying. This allows the site to be personalized to your needs.

data center *n.* A centralized repository for the storage, management, and dissemination of data and information organized around a particular body of knowledge. In a company, a data center is a term sometimes used to describe the central data processing facility and/or the group of people who manage the companies' data processing and server networks.

data dictionary *n.* A collection of descriptions of the data objects or items in a data model for the benefit of programmers and other who might need to refer to them. After identifying the required objects and relationships to other objects (called data modeling), these objects are given a name and description. The names are compiled into a data dictionary. This dictionary is referred to when the implementation of the data model takes place.

data element *n.* The smallest unit of data included in an EDI message. Often equates to a data processing field.

data element directory *n.* A listing of identified, named and described data elements, with a description of the allowable range of values. See data dictionary.

data encapsulation *n.* See encapsulation.

Data Encryption Standard (DES) *n.* An algorithm specified by NIST and the US National Security Agency to encipher and decipher data during transmission using a private (secret) key. See also encryption.

data flow chart *n.* A chart that illustrates the way in which specified data is handled by a computer program or system architecture.

data integrity *n.* An assurance that information can only be accessed or modified by those authorized to do so. Network administration measure to ensure data integrity include: maintaining current authorization levels for all users, documenting system administration procedures, parameters, and maintenance activities, and creating disaster recovery plans for power outages, server failure, and virus attacks.

data mart *n.* A repository of data gathered from operational data and other sources that is designed to serve a particular community of knowledge workers. The data may derive from an enterprise-wide database, data warehouse, or directory server. The principle behind the data mart is on meeting the specific demands of a particular group of knowledge users in terms of analysis, content, preparation, and ease-of-use. Users of a data mart can expect to have data presented in terms that are familiar.

data mining *v.* An analysis of data for relationships that have not been previously discovered. For example, data mining results may include associations of correlating purchases, sequences of purchases, recognition of a new demographic of buyers, and forecasting future buying patterns.

data mirroring *v.* Copying or mirroring data from a main or host computer to a backup (storage) machine.

data modeling *v.* An analysis of data objects that are used in a business or other context and the identification of the relationships among these data objects. Data modeling is generally the first step when designing in an object-oriented programming environment. The result of data modeling is having the ability to define the class that provides the templates for the program object. The Unified Modeling Language (UML) has become the standard modeling language.

Data Universal Numbering System (DUNS) *n.* A unique nine-character organization identification number assigned by Dun and Bradstreet. It's common for an organization to use this number as their EDI address (e.g. 183962349).

data warehousing *v.* The technology enabling data from multiple operational processing systems to be brought together into a single source, which can then be accessed and analyzed. The data can be both current and historical.

database *n.* A collection of data with a given structure for accepting, storing, and providing, on demand, data for multiple users.

database administrator (DBA) *n.* An individual who directs or performs all activities related to maintaining a database environment. Normal responsibilities may include designing, implementing, and maintaining the database system; establishing policies and procedures pertaining to the management, security, maintenance, and use of the database management system; and training employees in the database management and use.

database management system (DBMS) *n.* See database.

datagram *n.* A self-contained, independent entity of data carrying sufficient information to be routed from the source to the destination computer without reliance on earlier exchanges between this source and destination computer and the transporting network. Datagram is also known as a packet. Datagrams or packets are the message units that the Internet Protocol (IP) deals with and that the Internet transports.

DB2 *n.* A software application produced by IBM; a relational database management system for large computers, generally mainframe computers.

DC *n.* See Distribution Center.

DCAP *n.* See discounts, charges, allowances, and promotions.

dead freight *n.* Freight charges incurred by a shipper for space reserved but not used.

debit *n.* An entry on the left-hand side of an account in double-entry bookkeeping, showing an amount owed by the organization keeping the book. In the case of a bank account, a debit is an increase to the outflow of funds from the account.

debugging *v.* The process of locating and fixing errors (or bugs) in computer program code or the engineering of a hardware device. To debug a program or hardware device is to start with a problem, isolate the source of the problem, and then fix it.

decipher *v.* Also known as decrypt and decode; the process of converting ciphertext into the original, unencrypted plaintext.

decision-making unit (DMU) *n.* A group of individuals within an organization that decides which items the organization should buy. Commercial buying is undertaken by a group of people, rather than by individuals.

decryption *v.* The process of transforming an encrypted document back into its original form.

dedicated server *n.* Refers to the rental and exclusive use of a computer that may include a web server, related software, and connection to the Internet, housed on the web hosting company's premises. Usually a server that receives a large amount of traffic will require its own dedicated machine.

dedicated line *n.* A dedicated line is a telecommunications path between two points that is available 24 hours a day for use by a designated individual or company. It can be a physical path owned by the user or rented from a telephone company, in which case it is called a leased line. These types of lines are generally used with sensitive data, e.g. e-commerce transactions.

default *n.* The combining of requirements of two or more governmental units to obtain the benefits of volume purchases and/or reduction in administrative expenses.

defragmenter *n.* If a file is too large to store in a single location on a hard disk, it can be stored on the disk in many parts or fragments. The fragmentation isn't visible to the user, and the locations are kept track of by the system. A disk defragmenter is a utility that rearranges your fragmented files and the free space on your computer so that files are stored in complete units and free space is consolidated in one complete block. This also improves access time to files that are now complete.

delimiter *n.* A character used for the syntactical separation of data. Also known as a character separator. Common separators are commas or tab marks.

deliverable *n.* A report or product that must be delivered to the client by the contractor to satisfy contractual requirements.

delivered price *n.* A quoted price that includes the cost of packaging, insurance, and delivery to the destination given by the buyer.

demand chain management *n.* Same as supply chain management, but with emphasis on consumer pull vs. supplier push.

demand forecast *n.* An estimation of the future quantity demanded of a product in a market or industry.

demilitarized zone (DMZ) *n.* A computer or small network inserted as a neutral zone between a company's private network and the outside public network. It prevents outside users from getting direct access to a server that may have sensitive data on it. Typically, an organization's public web site is hosted somewhere in the DMZ.

demon *n.* See Daemon.

demurrage *n.* The detention of a ship, railroad, car or truck beyond a specified time for loading/unloading; the payment required and made for the delay.

Denial of Service (DoS) *n.* A denial of service attack is an incident in which a user or organization is deprived of services of a resource they would normally expect to have due to a type of security breach that does not usually result in the theft of information or other security loss. The most common denial of service attack is a buffer overflow attack, which is simply to send more traffic to a network address than the programmers who planned its data buffer anticipated someone might send. If a DoS attack was launched against a web site, an end-user would probably have a hard time accessing it due to the large amount of requests generated by the event.

deploy *v.* To deploy is to spread out or arrange strategically. In information technology, it generally means to upload to a designated area on a server.

deprecated *n.* A method or phrase that is still acceptable, but not recommended. This term is commonly used in programming languages when a previous feature has been replaced by something (presumably) better, however, your old code will still work with the new environment.

Deutschmark *n.* The standard monetary unit of Germany.

device driver *n.* A program that controls a particular type of device that is attached to your computer. There are device drivers for printers, monitors, CD-ROM drives, disk drives, etc. In Windows operating systems, a device driver file usually has a file name suffix of dll or exe.

DHCP *n.* See Dynamic Host Configuration Protocol (DHCP).

DHTML *n.* See Dynamic HTML (DHTML).

digital certificates *n.* Certificates issued by a Certificate Authority to enable an organization to exchange documents securely. It's issued by a Certificate Authority (CA). It contains your name, a serial number, expiration dates, a copy of the certificate holder's public key, and the digital signature of the certificate-issuing authority so that the recipient can verify that the certificate is real.

digital data storage *n.* A format for storing and backing up computer data on tape that evolved from the Digital Audio Tape (DAT) technology.

digital signature *n.* Data appended to, or a cryptographic transformation of, a data unit that allows a recipient of the data unit to prove the source and integrity of the data unit and protect against forgery (e.g. by the recipient). A digital signature can be used with any kind of message, whether it is encrypted or not, simply so the receiver can be sure of the sender's identity and the message arrived intact. See also encryption.

DirXML *n.* A software application developed by Novell to interact with their Directory Services platform. DirXML allows the administrator to manage all Directory Services from a single interface.

direct cost *n.* Any cost specifically identified as a final cost objective for a particular contract action. Includes cost factors such as direct labor and materials.

direct labor *n.* Labor required to complete a product or service. Includes fabrication, assembly, inspection and test for constructing an end product. Also, labor expended by contractor personnel in performing contractual requirements.

direct materials *n.* Includes raw materials, purchased parts and subcontracted items required to manufacture and assemble completed products. A direct material cost is the cost of material used in making a product.

direct procurement *n*. The purchasing of materials for use in manufacturing or distribution that are directly related to the finished product, goods, or services.

direct store delivery (DSD) *n*. A business operation where the supplier delivers the products directly to its customers retail stores rather than to their distribution center. DSD is generally used for products that have a limited shelf life (milk, vegetables).

disbursements *n*. In budgetary usage, gross disbursements represent the amount of checks, cash, or other payments issued, less refunds received. Usually a professional person, such as a banker, on behalf of a client makes disbursements.

discount *n*. A reduction in the price of goods below list price for various scenarios, usually when buying in bulk or for retailers who advertise a manufacturer's product.

discounts, charges, allowances, promotions (DCAP) *n*. The various modifications that can be made to a price in a price list without affecting the original value stored.

disk cache *n*. A mechanism to improve the time it takes to read from or write to a hard disk. The disk cache holds data that has recently been read.

disk operating system (DOS) *n*. An operating system, usually found on Microsoft platforms, where command-line functions can be executed.

dispatching rules *n*. Rules used to decide the priorities for fulfilling orders. Examples include FIFO (first-in-first-out), LIFO (last-in-first-out), and EDD (earliest-due-date).

distributed architecture *n.* A system of processing requests in which several computers are used at various locations within an organization instead of one central computer. Each computer has a specific operation or job to perform thus creating better efficiency for processing requests. Most E-Business systems have some type of distributed architecture usually separating the web server process, application logic, and database.

distributed file system *n.* A client/server based application that allows clients to access and process data stored on the server as if it were on their own computer. Essentially, a distributed file system creates a global directory for all users to access and write files to make available to the entire community.

Distributed Component Object Model (DCOM) *n.* A set of Microsoft concepts and program interfaces in which client program objects can request services from server program objects on other computers in a network. DCOM is based on the Component Object Model (COM), which provides a set of interfaces allowing clients and servers to communicate with the same computer. DCOM is the general equivalent to the Common Object Request Broker Architecture (CORBA) in terms of providing a set of distributed services.

distribution *n.* The allocation of goods to consumers by means of wholesalers and retailers.

distribution center (DC) *n.* A large automated warehouse designed to receive goods from various suppliers, take orders, fulfill them efficiently, and deliver goods to customers as quickly as possible.

distribution channel *n.* A network of organizations necessary to distribute goods or services from the manufacturers to the consumers; the channel therefore consists of manufacturers, distributors, wholesalers, and retailers.

DLL *n.* See dynamic link library (DLL).

DMZ *n.* See demilitarized zone (DMZ).

DNS *n.* See Domain Name System (DNS).

Document Object Model (DOM) *n.* A programming interface specification developed by the World Wide Web Consortium (W3C); it allows a programmer to create and modify HTML and XML pages to be treated as a programmable object. As objects, documents can carry with them the object-oriented procedures called methods.

Document Type Definition (DTD) *n.* A specification for an XML document that identifies what the markup means. By accompanying the XML document with a DTD, any location that has a DTD reader will have the ability to process the document and display or print it as intended.

Domain Name System (DNS) *n.* The Internet naming scheme that consists of a hierarchical sequence of names, from the most specific to the most general (left to right), separated by dots, for example nic.ddn.mil. It is a distributed database system used to map host names to Internet Protocol address and vice versa. See also TCP/IP.

downloading *v.* The electronic transfer of information from one computer to another, generally from a larger computer to a smaller one, such as a microcomputer.

downstream *n.* Sometimes referred to as "downstream the supply chain." The direction in which materials flow (e.g. a customer will always be downstream from its suppliers).

down time *n.* The period during which a computer or network of computers are out of action, usually because of a fault or for maintenance work.

Drachma *n.* The standard monetary unit of Greece.

driver *n.* A program that interacts with a particular device or different piece of software. The driver contains the information needed to communicate to the device or software. Drivers on a Window's system usually have the DLL suffix.

drop ship *n.* See Drop shipment.

drop shipment *n.* Merchandise that is shipped by a manufacturer directly to a customer in response to the seller who collects orders but does not maintain an inventory.

DSD *n.* See direct store delivery (DSD).

DUNS *n.* See Data Universal Numbering System (DUNS).

DUNS number *n.* See Data Universal Numbering System (DUNS).

dutch auction *n.* An auction sale in which the auctioneer starts by calling a very high price and reduces it until a bid is received.

dynamic *adj.* Capable of change; usually in an information technology environment, dynamic refers to data that is derived from a data source; e.g. a database or directory server.

Dynamic HTML (DHTML) *n.* An all-inclusive term for a combination of new HTML tags and options that allows you to create web pages, which are more animated and more responsive to user interaction than previous versions of HTML. Much of the HTML 4.0 standard has DHTML capabilities. Examples include moving text, layers of color, and cascading style sheets.

Dynamic Host Configuration Protocol (DHCP) *n.* A communications protocol that allows the assignment of Internet Protocol (IP) addresses to be automated. This type of scenario is common when users dial in to a company's internal network. There may be a block of 200 addresses allocated to 1000 users with the assumption that all 1000 users will not be logged on at the same time and 200 being the maximum number of users to dial in.

dynamic IP address *n.* An IP address that is allocated from a DHCP server, usually during a dial-up session. These are useful for users with mobile devices that require an IP address.

Dynamic Link Library (DLL) *n.* A collection of small programs that can be called by larger programs which ultimately save space in a computers random access memory (RAM). If the DLL file is needed, it is loaded into RAM and executed.

Ee

E-Business *n.* Electronic business; the process of buying, selling, servicing and collaborating with business partners. Large corporations who are transferring their old paper business to electronic forms can realize huge cost savings.

E-Outsourcing *n.* The process of buying information technology products and services that previously were the responsibility of individuals within the organization. For example, an organization might hire an outside security firm to install and maintain a firewall to protect their local area network. One of the attractive advantages of e-outsourcing is the hiring of outside vendors to act as the IT department, which allows internal employees more time to concentrate on core activities (e.g. activities which generate revenue).

E-Procurement *n.* Electronic procurement is the processes making up the procurement operation that is done electronically and paper-free. The words "e-buying, e-purchasing, and e-procurement" are sometimes used interchangeably, but e-procurement covers the entire operation of procurement and not just the buying process (e.g. approval process, shipping, etc.). E-procurement includes a company's requisitioning, purchasing, transportation, warehousing, and in-bound receiving processes. E-Procurement is a multi-stage process that begins with a user logging into a computer application and ending when the invoice for the products selected is paid.

Advantages of an electronic procurement process (compared to a paper-based system):

1. All employees can participate in the purchasing process due to ease-of-use; self-service on the internet. Corporate procurement capability is available to anyone with a web browser.
2. A sharp reduction in order-processing costs and cycle times. The products and services ordered should be delivered faster because the process is more efficient.
3. A company's E-Procurement system can communicate to other application system's rather than storing redundant data (e.g. E-Procurement application communicating to an Accounting application).
4. It brings focus to the function of procurement and the importance of cost-saving.
5. It attempts to limit maverick buying practices, for example buying office supplies with your corporate credit card at a local store--buying at a price that wasn't pre-negotiated.

It's estimated that for each dollar a company earns on the sale of a product, it spends about $0.50-0.60 on goods and services. It's obvious that a key aspect of a company's E-Procurement strategy is to better manage a firm's operational costs. Billions of dollars are wasted every year in inefficient procurement practices. The bottom-line impact of margin improvement afforded by E-Procurement is significant--especially when comparing this with revenue-focused activities.

For example, according to CFO Magazine's annual survey on sales, general, and administrative costs (SG&A), "slicing SG&A by $1 has the same bottom-line effect as boosting sales by $13" and "cutting 1 percent from SG&A will improve earnings by 2.3 percent."

early adopter *n*. An organization who purchases a new product or implements a new concept soon after it has been introduced, but after the innovators. Early adopters of E-Procurement could be found in the late 1990s.

EBIT *n*. Abbreviation for earnings before interest and tax.

EbXML *n*. An acronym for Electronic Business Extensible Markup Language; a new XML standard meant to take the place of Electronic Data Interchange (EDI). The United Nations body for Trade Facilitation and Electronic Business Information Standards (UN/CEFACT) and the Organization for the Advancement of Structured Information Standards (OASIS) launched the project. The project is built on three concepts: provide an infrastructure that ensures data communication interoperability; provide a semantics framework that ensures commercial interoperability; and provide a mechanism that allows enterprises to find each other, agree to become trading partners and conduct business with each other.

ECMAScript *n*. A standardized script language similar to Netscape's Javascript and Microsoft's Jscript. An object-orientated scripting language and is a core-language for programming within documents. The vision of the ECMAScript project is the blending together of Microsoft's and Netscape's implementations into one standard language.

economic price adjustment *n*. An alteration permitted and specified by contract provision for the upward or downward revision of a stated contract price based upon the occurrence of certain contingencies that are defined in the contract.

ECXpert *n*. A Sun One product; e-commerce software that transmits business documents and messages between buyers and suppliers.

EDI *n.* See Electronic Data Interchange (EDI).

EDI Address *n.* The published address to which messages (EDI) for a particular organization can be sent.

EDI Interchange *n.* A data transmission structured in accordance with an EDI standard and containing one or more (usually related) messages (EDI) sent to one trading partner.

EDI Transaction Set *n.* An electronic business document comprised of a set of predefined EDI segments, which begin with a header and end with a trailer. The transaction set normally has three sections: a header section of data fields referring to the entire transaction set, a detail section of data fields referencing individual line items, and a summary section called a trailer.

EDIFACT *n.* See Electronic Data Interchange For Administration, Commerce and Transport.

EDIFACT directory *n.* A listing of the building blocks (data elements, data segments and messages) comprising the EDIFACT standard.

EDM *n.* See Electronic Document Management (EDM).

effective competition *n.* A market condition which exists when two or more contractors, acting independently, actively compete for an agency's business in a manner which ensures that the agency will be offered the lowest price or best technical design to meet its minimum needs.

Efficient Consumer Response (ECR) *n.* A general business strategy in which the retailer, distributor and supplier trading partners work closely together to eliminate excess costs from the supply chain.

Efficient Healthcare Consumer Response (EHCR) *n.* A specific business strategy adopted by the healthcare industry. Trading partners use technology to effectively manage the flow of business data in an effort to have the right product and services at the right time and for the right price.

EFT *n.* See Electronic Funds Transfer (EFT).

EFTA *n.* Abbreviation for European Free Trade Association.

EFTPOS *n.* See Electronic Funds Transfer At Point Of Sale (EFTPOS).

EHCR *n.* See Efficient Healthcare Consumer Response (EHCR).

electronic bulletin board *n.* A shared file where users can enter information for other users to read or download. Many bulletin boards are set up according to general topics and are accessible throughout a network.

Electronic Data Interchange (EDI) *n.* A trade exchange system that replaces common business forms such as purchase orders, shipping forms, invoices, etc., with a computer-based communications and record keeping system.

Electronic Data Interchange For Administration, Commerce and Transport (EDIFACT) *n.* Also known as UN/EDIFACT, it is one of the two international standards describing the syntax of EDI transmissions. EDIFACT is administered by a working party (WP.4) of the United Nations Economic Commission for Europe (UN/ECE). The EDIFACT syntax rules have been published by the International Standards Organization (ISO) as ISO9735.

Electronic Document Management (EDM) *n.* The capture, storage, and retrieval of electronic images of documents.

Electronic Funds Transfer (EFT) *n.* The electronic transfer of funds from one account to another.

Electronic Funds Transfer At Point Of Sale (EFTPOS) *n.* The electronic transfer of funds from one account to another done at the point of sale of a product. Involves the transfer of funds from a buyer's account to the sellers account.

electronic mail (e-mail) *n.* The electronic transfer of business or personal information, in normal language, between individuals. See SMTP.

electronic signature *n.* A form of authentication that lets you identify and validate a transaction by means of an authorization code.

Emacs *n.* Derived from Editing Macros; a popular text editor used mainly on UNIX-based systems. Like other UNIX text editors, emacs provides typed commands and special key combinations that let you add, delete, insert, and manipulate words.

employment costs *n.* The expense incurred in employing personnel. It includes wages, salaries, bonuses, incentive payments, and pension payments.

encapsulation *n.* The inclusion of one thing within another thing so that the included thing is not apparent. Decapsulation is the removal or the making apparent of a thing previously encapsulated. A common term in object-oriented programming, encapsulation in this context is the inclusion with a program object of all the resources needed for the project to function.

encryption *n.* The process of transforming data into an unintelligible form in such a way that the original data either cannot be reconstructed or can be reconstructed only by using a decryption process. My smartass editor believes the preceding sentence is an example of encryption. See also algorithm, cipher, cryptographic algorithm, public key encryption, and secret key encryption.

end-to-end security *n.* Security which is applied at the end-points of a transmission process with no interaction by intermediate nodes.

enterprise *n.* An entire firm or organization that uses information technology. The term is generally used as an adjective denoting that the entire organization uses a particular component (e.g. enterprise email system).

enterprise JavaBeans (EJB) *n.* An architecture for setting up program components, written in the Java programming language. Enterprise JavaBeans offers the enterprise the advantage of being able to change at the server rather than having to update each individual computer with a client whenever a new program component is changed or added.

enterprise resource planning (ERP) *n.* A term for a broad set of activities supported by application software that helps an organization manage the important parts of the business, including product planning, parts purchasing, maintaining inventories, interacting with suppliers, providing customer service, and tracking orders.

entity *n.* A label used to identify units, whether concrete things or abstract ideas, that have no ready name or label. Commonly used when diagramming an architecture on a white board.

entity-relationship diagram *n.* A data-modeling technique that creates a graphical representation of the entities, and the relationship between entities, within an information system.

envelope *n.* A structured set of fields that contain addressing, error checking and other administrative information necessary to ensure the complete and accurate transmission of an EDI transmission. See also Electronic Data Interchange and Enveloping.

enveloping *v.* An EDI management software function that groups all documents of the same type, or functional group, and bound for the same destination into an electronic envelope. An electronic envelope can be compared to paper envelope easily. Just as you can stuff an Invoice and Purchase Order into a paper envelope, you can do the same thing with an electronic envelope (different documents separated by pre-defined standards).

EOM *n.* Stands for "end of message." Commonly used when people exchange email with short messages, they'll conclude with the EOM acronym.

ergonomics *n.* The study of physical and psychological aspects of work; it is primarily concerned with designing jobs and work environments that are safe and efficient. Increased attention has been dedicated to safe office environments due to injuries resulting from prolonged periods of computer use and typing.

ERP *n.* See enterprise resource planning (ERP).

ERS *n.* See Evaluated Receipt Settlement (ERS).

escalation *n.* Determination of price adjustments based on increases or decreases to indexes specifically identified in the contract.

escalation clause *n.* A contract provision which permits the adjustment of contract prices by an amount or percent if certain specified contingencies occur, such as changes in the vendor's raw material or labor costs.

ethernet *n.* A method of networking computers in a Local Area Network (LAN). Ethernet can handle around 10 million bits per second. See also bandwidth.

EU *n.* See European Union.

Euro *n.* The currency unit to be used by the European Monetary Union.

European Union *n.* Fifteen nations that have joined together to form an economic community with some common goals. These nations include Belgium, Denmark, France, Germany, Greece, Ireland, Italy, Luxembourg, the Netherlands, Portugal, Spain, the UK, Austria, Finland, and Sweden. However, the UK still uses its own currency, not the Euro.

Evaluated Receipt Settlement (ERS) *n.* A business strategy that allows the customer to pay its supplier based on matching the material received with the advance ship notice. It means that the supplier does not send its customer an invoice.

ex gratia *n.* Latin for 'as of grace'; it denotes a payment made out of gratitude, kindness, etc., rather than to fulfill a legal obligation.

exception *n.* A term used interchangeably with error. Many programming languages have the ability to handle exceptions. This means that a programmer will predict where errors might occur, and write code to handle these errors without the end-user knowing it, or at least produce an error message that is readable. Applications may produce "Exception Reports", which is a recorded list of errors that occurred in a duration of time.

exception-based processing *n.* Applications that automatically highlight particular events or results that fall outside pre-determined parameters. This saves considerable effort by automatically finding problems and alerting the right people.

excise duty *n.* A duty or tax levied on certain goods, such as alcohol and tobacco products.

exclusive distribution *n.* A situation in which a distributor carries the products of one manufacturer and not those of competitors; this may give the distributor exclusive rights to distribute the company's products in certain regions.

exit strategy *n.* Short-term strategy on how to exit a venture on acceptable terms. This might include a buy-out from a larger company, initial public offering, or a set time-schedule for key employees to leave the organization.

expenditure *n.* A charge against available funds, evidenced by a voucher or a claim. Expenditure represents the actual payment of funds.

Extended Binary Coded Decimal Interchange Code (EBCDIC) *n.* A coding system for representing characters, defined by IBM and used in the IBM and compatible mainframe environment. In an EBCDIC file, each letter or number is represented with an 8-bit binary number (a string of eight 0's or 1's).

extensible *n.* A term to describe something, such as a program, programming language, or protocol, that is designed so that users can extend its capabilities. The primary feature of the extensible markup language (XML) is having the ability to create your own markup language.

Extensible Markup Language (XML) *n.* XML is a markup

language for documents containing structured information. Structured information contains both content (words, pictures, etc.) and some indication of what role that content plays (for example, content in a section heading has a different meaning from content in a footnote, which means something different than content in a figure caption or content in a database table, etc.). Almost all documents have some structure. A markup language is a mechanism to identify structures in a document. The XML specification defines a standard way to add markup to documents.
(taken from xml.com)

Extensible Stylesheet Language (XSL) *n.* A language for creating a style template that describes how a xml document will be presented to a user. XSL was based on the Document Style Semantics and Specification Language (DSSSL) and the Cascading Style Sheet, level 1 (CSS1) standards.

extension *n.* A file name extension allows a file's format to be described as part of its name so that users can quickly understand the type of file it is without having to open or try to use it. It also helps an application program recognize whether a file is a type that it can work with.

extranet *n.* A private network that uses the Internet Protocol and the public telecommunication system to securely share part of a business operations with suppliers, vendors, partners, customers, or other businesses. An extranet can be viewed as part of a company's intranet that is extended to users outside the company.

eye candy *n.* A term used in information technology for visual properties displayed on computer screens that are aesthetically appealing or attention getting. Generally, eye candy refers to superficial elements of an application that are not functional in nature.

Eyrir *n.* A monetary unit of Iceland.

Ff

FA *n.* See Functional Acknowledgment.

facilities contract *n.* Provides for the procurement, construction, and installation of facilities or the use, maintenance, management, accountability, or disposition of facilities.

fatal exception *n.* A computer error message. It usually indicates a situation requiring the program responsible for the exception be closed or shut down. When it occurs, the operating system has no other recourse but to shut down the application, and in some instances, its own operating system.

Federal Acquisition Regulation (FAR) *n.* The primary regulation used by all Federal agencies in their acquisition of supplies and services with appropriated funds. It is issued within applicable laws under the joint authorities of the Administrator of General Services, the Secretary of Defense, and the Administrator for the National Aeronautics and Space Administration, under the broad policy guidelines of the Administrator, Office of Federal Procurement Policy, Office of Management and Budget.

FGI *n.* See Finished Goods Inventory.

field selling *v.* Non-retail selling that takes place outside the employer's place of business, usually at a potential customer's premises.

FIFO *n.* Abbreviation for first-in-first-out.

file system *n.* A way in which files are named and where they are placed logically for storage and retrieval. Most operating systems have file systems in which files are placed somewhere in a hierarchical structure.

File Transfer Protocol (FTP) *n.* File Transfer Protocol allows a user to transfer files electronically from remote computers back to the user's computer. Part of the **TCP/IP** software suite.

fill rate *n.* The percent of orders shipped within an order due date.

final invoice *n.* An invoice containing any missing information from previous invoices and states the full amount still owed for the goods.

Financial Products Markup Language (FpML) *n.* A business information exchange standard based on the extensible markup language (XML) that enables business-to-business over-the-counter financial transactions over the internet. Due to an extensible structure and evolving technologies, companies can electronically structure and negotiate the terms of an OTC contract.

finger *n.* A UNIX program that tells you the name associated with an email address or a user that is currently logged on to the system.

Finished Goods Inventory (FGI) *n.* The area of an assembly plant designated for finished products.

firewall *n.* A computer system usually inserted between a company's infrastructure or local area network and the internet to filter incoming

---

traffic, to try to eliminate viral infection, and to restrict the access of hackers to the system. It may create a bottleneck in the transmission of data to and from the system.

firm offer *n*. An offer to sell goods that remains valid for a stated period. For example, an 'offer firm for 48 hours' binds the seller to sell if the buyer accepts the offer within 48 hours.

first mover *n*. A company that aims to gain a superior market position by being the first to establish itself in a given market. Examples of first movers include Amazon.com, Ebay, and Yahoo. Although there is considerable competition in all of these industries, their easy-to-remember brand name and maturity has enabled them to dominate the internet marketplace.

fiscal year *n*. The 12 months between one annual settlement of financial accounts and the next; a term used for budgeting, etc. The fiscal year for the U.S. Government is October 1 to September 30.

fixed exchange rate *n*. A rate of exchange between one currency and another that is fixed by government and maintained by that government buying or selling its currency to support or depress its currency.

fixed length *n*. A data field or record within an e-business document that has a predefined number of characters. For example, the first line of an EDI document known as the ISA header has fixed length fields detailing address information.

fixed price contract *n*. A type of contract that provides for a firm price or, under appropriate circumstances, for an adjustable price for the supplies or services being procured.

flaming *n*. An e-mail or newsgroup posting that points out the negative or un-intelligent aspects of another individual or organization. Often times, an employee will send "flaming e-mails" to other employees to express dissatisfaction and disillusionment with them and/or the organization.

flat file *n*. A text file with a fixed-record length. They are often used to exchange data between an EDI business application and an interface to another system. Generally, these types of files don't have delimiters. See also ASCII.

float *n*. The time required for documents, payments, etc. to get from one trading partner to another.

Florin *n*. The standard monetary unit of Aruba.

flow control *n*. The management of data flow between computers or devices in a network so that the data can be handled at an efficient pace. Too much data arriving before a device can handle it causes data overflow, meaning the data is either lost or must be retransmitted.

flowchart *n*. A graphic representation of a program sequence, work or manufacturing process, organization chart, or similar structure.

FMIS *n*. Acronym for Financial Management Information System.

font *n*. A set of printable or displayable text character's in a specific style or size. The type design for a set of fonts is the typeface and variations of this design form the typeface family.

forecasting *n*. Predicting sales and use of products so the correct amounts can be ordered.

Forint *n*. The standard monetary unit of Hungary.

format *n*. To format a hard disk or floppy disk is to set up space divisions on the disk and initiate a space allocation table that will know how to reach each bit of data that may be stored there later.

FORTRAN *n.* Acronym for FORmula TRANslation, a computer programming language used for mathematical and scientific work that was dominant during the 1950s through the 1970s.

forward auction *n.* An auction with one seller and many potential buyers. Similar to model auction houses such as Sotheby's.

forward DNS lookup *n.* Using an internet domain name to find an IP address; the opposite of reverse DNS lookup (using an IP address to find a domain name).

FpML *n.* See Financial Products Markup Language (FpML).

frame relay *n.* A communications service designed for cost-efficient data transmission for traffic between local area networks and between end-points in a wide area network. Frame relay puts data in variable-size units called a form and leaves any necessary error correction up to the end-points. It's often used to connect local area networks with major backbones.

frames *n.* An extension of a web browser that allows multiple HTML pages to be presented on one page. When a user requests a web page that uses frames, it calls the "master" page which defines the frames; and the multiple pages are called from the master.

Free Software Foundation *n.* Founded in 1983 by MIT professor Richard Stallman with the goal of developing an operating system (called GNU) and sharing it freely with the general public without copying or modifying stipulations.

freight bill *n.* The bill from the carrier for costs incurred by shipping.

Freight on Board (FOB) *n*. Specifies the location where title to the goods passes from the supplier to the buyer. For example, a supplier who agrees to pay costs FOB will only pay freight costs to a pre-specified location and the buyer pays any charges beyond the FOB location.

freight note *n*. An invoice from a shipowner to a shipper showing the amount of freight due on a shipment of goods.

freight terms *n*. An agreement between buyer and supplier companies on how an order should be taxed and how the carrier is to be paid. Freight terms can be applied to an entire order or to a group of lines that have the same freight terms.

front-end *n*. An application that users interact with directly. Generally it refers to a web browser (client application) or the first tier of a distributed architecture (e.g. web server).

FTP See File Transfer Protocol (FTP).

fully-qualified domain name *n*. A URL name that fully identifies the server program that an Internet request is addressed to (e.g. imus.msnbc.com).

functional acknowledgement *n*. An EDI message acknowledging the receipt of a transmission and notifying the sender of whether or not it matched the syntax expected by the recipient's translator. For example, a customer will send a Purchase Order (850) to a supplier, and the supplier's EDI system will generate a functional acknowledgment (997) to send back to the customer indicating they have received the purchase order.

functional group *n*. One or more messages of same type contained

---

within an EDI interchange.

functional requirements *n.* Identification of the business or administrative tasks that need to be met for an E-Business application.

Gg

GAAP *n.* Abbreviation for Generally Accepted Accounting Principles.

Gantt chart *n.* A chart presenting a planned activity as horizontal bands against a background of dates. This is a graphical representation found in Microsoft Project and other project-planning software. Henry L. Gantt invented it in 1917.

gap analysis *n.* A methodical tabulation of all the known requirements of a project cross-listed with all known existing features already completed. Such an analysis will show any gaps and therefore point where concentration should be focused.

garbage *n.* The data that has been placed in random access memory (RAM) space obtained from the operating system that is no longer needed.

garbage collecting *n.* The recovery of pooled computer storage that is being used by a program when that program no longer needs the storage. Java has a built-in garbage collecting system allowing the programmer not to write code for it.

gateway *n.* A connection between two networks that allows data (e.g. in the form of electronic messages) on one to be routed through to the other.

gb *n.* See Gigabyte (GB).

Gbps Billions of bits per second; a measure of bandwidth on a data transmission medium. Other bandwidth speeds include Mbps (millions of bits per second) and Kbps (thousands of bits per second).

GEIS *n.* General Electric Information Services; consulting company with a specialty in electronic commerce.

Generalized Markup Language (GML) *n.* An IBM document formatting language that describes a document in terms of its organization structure and content parts and their relationship to each other.

generic mapping *n.* A study of multiple maps before designing a simple EDI transaction set with the goal of fitting multiple trading partners' requirements for a transaction set into one.

generic top-level domain name (gTLD) *n.* A domain name of an Internet address that identifies it generically as associated with some domain class, such as .net (for Internet service providers), .org (for non-profit organizations) and .edu (for educational institutions).

GIF *n.* See Graphics Interchange Format (GIF).

gigabyte (GB) *n.* A thousand megabytes.

gigahertz (GHz) *n.* A unit of alternating current or electromagnetic wave frequency equal to one thousand million hertz. Personal computer clock speeds are increasing every year as the technology advances, and reached the 1 GHz point in March 2000, with a processor from AMD.

GIMP *n*. The GNU Image Manipulation Program (GIMP); a freely available open source application for creating and manipulating graphic images that run on UNIX-based operating systems. GIMP is comparable to Adobe's Photoshop and Illustrator applications.

glass ceiling *n*. Invisible artificial barriers that can limit the career advancement of employees, particularly women and members of minority groups. While laws in most countries prohibit this type of barrier, they are not always followed.

global information system *n*. An organized collection of telecommunications equipment, computer software, data, and personnel designed to capture, store, update, manipulate, analyze, and display data from a broad range of information about worldwide business activities.

globalization *n*. The internationalization of products and services by large organizations.

GMAIC *n*. General Merchandise and Apparel Implementation Committee. This committee operates under the guidance of the Uniform Code Council (UCC) and implements Universal Product Code (UPC, e.g. bar codes) standards for the retail industry.

GNOME *n*. GNU Network Object Model Environment; a graphical user interface and set of desktop applications for users of UNIX-based operating systems. Similar to Microsoft's Window's operating system, but several other desktop appearances are available to the end-user.

GNU *n*. A UNIX-based operating system developed by the Free Software Foundation. The GNU project was started in 1983 by Richard Stallman and others. The GNU applications come with source code that can be copied, modified, and redistributed.

godown *n*. See warehouse.

golden handcuffs *n.* Financial incentives offered to key staff to persuade them to remain with an organization; usually in the form of stock-option that vest after a certain period of time.

golden parachute *n.* A clause in the employment contract of a senior executive in a company that provides for financial and other benefits if the executive is fired or decides to leave as the result of a takeover or change of ownership.

Gourde *n.* The standard monetary unit of Haiti.

granularity *n.* The relative size, scale, level of detail, or depth of penetration that characterizes an object or activity. In the information technology context, it can refer to the level of hierarchy of objects or actions, the detail of photograph, or to the amount of information that is supplied in describing a person's age.

Graphical User Interface (GUI) *n.* A web-based interface that allows users to perform user tasks. For example, the graphical user interface of Amazon.com allows the shopper to search for items easily.

Graphics Interchange Format (GIF) *n.* A format for graphics files. Commonly used for transfer of graphics files due to its use of data compression that makes the files smaller and the transfers faster; a common image format on the World Wide Web.

grep *n.* A UNIX command which is used to search one or more files for a given character string or pattern. For example, a user can enter this on a command line:

% grep hello index.html

hello specifies the string to search for on each line and *index.html* specifies the file to search. The output of the search is automatically displayed below the command prompt.

% ps -ef | grep httpd

The above example is more common; the user is executing a detailed process summary (ps) and piped the grep command to search for the httpd process. Ask UNIX users what their favorite and most useful command is and many will say grep.

grey market *n.* Any market for goods that are in short supply. It differs from a black market because it is legal; a black market is not.

GUI *n.* Graphical User Interface; generally the application screens that a user will interact with.

guilder *n.* The standard monetary unit of the Netherlands, the Antilles, and Surinam.

Hh

hacker *n.* An individual with an understanding of the structure and operation of computer networks, who deliberately breaks into confidential systems. Also known as a cracker, although this term generally refers to an individual who attempts to break into confidential systems for the benefit of the client or software manufacturer.

half-duplex *n.* A type of internet transmission that allows data to go in both directions on a single carrier, but not at the same time. For example, a workstation that has half-duplex transmission can send data on the line and then immediately receive data on the line from the same direction in which the data was just transmitted.

Handheld Device Markup Language (HDML) *n.* Similar to the Wireless Markup Language (WML), HDML was developed by Unwired Planet (now phone.com) and allows text portions of web pages to be presented on cellular phones and personal digital assistants (PDA) via wireless access.

hard currency *n.* A currency that is commonly accepted throughout the world. Holdings of hard currency are valued because of their universal purchasing power; examples of hard currency are US dollars, and British Pound Sterling.

hard disk *n.* A type of computer memory that uses a magnetic disk enclosed in a sealed compartment to store information.

hardcode *n.* A programming term that refers to using an explicit name rather than a symbol for something that is likely to change at a later time. The inability to customize an application is often blamed on components that are hardcoded (e.g. the US dollar sign '$' hardcoded on the order summary screen).

hardware *n.* The physical equipment (servers, workstations, computer cable, etc.) that is used in data processing and server hosts.

Hardware Abstraction Layer (HAL) *n.* A layer of programming that allows a computer operating system to interact with hardware devices at a general or abstract level rather than at a detailed hardware level.

hash functions *n.* A computation that reduces a large number of bits to a smaller number of bits in such a way that all of the original bits influence the outcome of the computation. See hashing.

hashing *n.* A transformation of characters into a shorter fixed-length value or key that represents the original string. Hashing is commonly used to speed up the performance of a database by optimizing index and retrieve operations.

head hunter *n.* Consultants that specialize in finding suitable managers and executives for a firm, or finding suitable jobs for executives who want a change.

header 1. *n.* The segment of an EDI document that indicates the start of an entity that is to be transmitted; control structures of a document. 2. *n.* In email, the header is the part of the message that describes the originator, the addressee and other recipients, message priority level, and other administrative details of the mail.

header area *n.* The transaction set header area of an EDI document that contains preliminary information that pertains to the entire document, such as date, company name, address, terms, etc.

HEDIC *n.* Healthcare EDI Corporation; a non-profit organization that was formed in 1991 to provide EDI education and to assist in the roll out of EDI among hospitals and their suppliers.

help desk *n.* A place that a user of information technology can call to get help with a computer-related problem. A related term is call center, a place that customers call to place orders, track shipments, and get help with products, etc.

heterogeneous *adj.* In information technology it describes an environment that may have many different components, usually software products by different manufacturers. Due to standards and common protocols, the different products are able to communicate to each other.

heuristic *n.* The process of knowing by trying rather than by following some pre-established formula. Many e-procurement projects could be described as heuristic due to the immaturity of the products, consultants, and business processes.

hexadecimal *n.* A numbering system containing 16 sequential numbers as base units before adding a new position for the next number. The hexadecimal numbers are 0-9 and the letters A-F. A common usage of hexadecimal numbers is defining a color on a web page. See the appendix for a table comparing binary, decimal, and hexadecimal numbers.

hiccup *n.* A non-recurring information technology problem of an undetermined cause that usually does not cause a significant disruption of work or activity. A hiccup is similar to a glitch, but is usually less serious.

high level *adj.* See high-level language.

high-level language 1. *n.* A type of computer programming language that is designed to reflect the needs of the programmer rather than the capabilities of the computer. They use abstract data and control structures, and symbolic names for variables. Examples include C and BASIC. 2. *n.* A non-specific description of how a computer program or system really works; a generic discussion.

hijacking *n.* A type of network security attack in which a hacker takes control of a computer or communication between users. DNS hijacking is another type where a user attacks an organization's DNS records to take over a domain name.

HIN *n.* Health Industry Number; a unique number used to identify all healthcare entities.

home page *n.* A graphical document that acts as an entry point to the World Wide Web. Set in a page format, it provides link access to related menus and files.

hook *n.* A place where an interface is provided that allows a programmer to insert customized programming for additional capabilities. Most e-procurement applications will provide hooks for such capabilities as price schedules, shipping, and time-card customization.

hop *n.* In a packet-switching network, it's the trip a packet takes from one router to another point in the network. On the internet, the number of hops a packet has taken toward its destination is kept in the packet header and is called a hop-count.

horizontal hub *n.* A hub which cuts across many industries, usually providing a common service such as product data storage.

horizontal markets *n.* Similar to horizontal hub, potential customers who reside in different industries. 'Horizontal Play' is also used in the same context.

host *n.* Any computer on a network that is a repository for services available to other computers on the network.

hot swap *n.* The replacement of a hard drive, CD-ROM drive, power supply, or other device with a similar device while the computer system using it is still turned on or in operation.

HP-UX *n.* A UNIX-based operating system manufactured by Hewlett-Packard specifically for the HP 9000 series of business servers.

HTML *n.* See Hypertext Markup Language (HTML).

HTTP *n.* Hypertext Transfer Protocol; a protocol for exchanging files (text, graphic, images, sound, video, and other files) on the World Wide Web. An essential part of HTTP includes the idea that files can contain references to other files whose selection will produce additional transfer requests. An HTTP daemon is a program that is designed to wait for HTTP requests and handle them when they arrive.

hub 1. *n.* An organization that provides a large number of trading services. 2. *n.* A common connection point for devices in a network.

humanware *n.* Hardware and software that emphasizes user capability and the design of the user interface. This type of software is specifically designed to interact with users, including speech recognition and applications that work with the disabled.

Hypertext Markup Language (HTML) *n.* A markup language, consisting of text interspersed with a few basic formatting tags, used to create documents on the World Wide Web.

Hypertext Transfer Protocol *n.* See HTTP.

Ii

I/O *n.* See input/output (I/O).

IAS *n.* Abbreviation for International Accounting Standards.

ICANN *n.* Internet Corporation for Assigned Names and Numbers is a private non-profit corporation responsible for IP address space allocation, protocol parameter assignment, domain name system management, and root server system management functions.

icon *n.* A pictorial representation of a command, function, or piece of data used in computer applications. Also used on the World Wide Web as hypertext in place of normal textual links.

identifier *n.* A character or groups of characters used to identify or name an item of data and possibly to indicate certain EDI properties of that data.

IIS *n.* See Internet Information Server (IIS).

image map *n.* A graphic image defined so that a user can click on different areas of the image and be linked to different destinations. You produce an image map by defining an area in terms of their x and y coordinates which are horizontal and vertical distances relative from the left-hand corner of the image. With each set of coordinates, you specify a URL or web address that will be linked to when the user clicks on that area.

IMAP *n.* See Internet Message Access Protocol (IMAP).

imperial units *n.* A system of units formerly widely used in the United Kingdom and the rest of the English-speaking world. It includes the pound (lb), quart (qt), hundredweight (cwt), and ton (ton). Metric units have largely replaced these units, although imperial units persist in some contexts.

impressions *n.* The number of times that an element (such as an image) of a page has been viewed by an individual browser. Often used to count Internet ad placements.

impulse buying *n.* The buying of a product by a consumer without previous intention and almost always without evaluation of competing brands. Also known as maverick purchasing.

in bond *n.* Delivery terms for goods that are available for immediate delivery but are held in a bonded warehouse. Usually the buyer has to pay the cost of any customs duty due, the cost of loading from the warehouse, and any further costs.

incompatibility *n.* The inability of one computer system or application to handle data and programs produced for a different type of computer or application.

incubator *n.* A facility for a startup company with a direction and enough capital to get out of the garage, but not quite enough to get off the ground. Often, groups of entrepreneurs benefit from shared services and shared knowledge in an incubator, which can provide administrative support, telephones, copy machines, and shared capital. Originally sponsored by universities, government, or economic development groups, the most successful incubators today are part of a venture capital organization, or function under the auspices of a wealthy investor.

independent portal *n.* See buying portal.

indirect procurement *n.* The purchasing of any product or service that does not result directly in the finished good. For example, the purchase of office supplies, computers, furniture, and travel requirements would be considered a part of indirect procurement. Usually, more than 2/3 of a purchasing budget goes to these types of transactions.

inertia selling *v.* A form of selling in which goods are sent to a potential customer on a sale-or-return bases, without his prior consent or knowledge. This method is especially prevalent with book and record clubs.

infomediary *n.* A web site that provides specialized information on behalf of producers of goods and services and their potential customers. The term is made up of *information* and *intermediary*. Gathering information and adding services to a web site has become increasingly popular. This type of service is common for sites that offer information for businesses about suppliers.

Information and Content Exchange (ICE) *n.* An XML-based standard protocol for electronic business-to-business asset management which defines an architecture and a common language that can be used as a means of automating Web content syndication for publishing and e-commerce uses. It enables the automation of data supplying, exchanging, updating, and controlling without requiring the supplier to manually package content, or to maintain knowledge about the structure of the recipient web sites. Members of the ICE Authoring Group include Adobe, Microsoft, Sun Microsystems, and Vignette (among others). ICE version 1.1 was released in June 2000.

information technology (IT) *n*. A broad term which describes the use of computers and other electronic means to process and distribute information.

inheritance *adj*. A programming term, it's the concept that when a class or object is defined, any subclass that is defined can inherit the definitions of one or more general classes. This tends to speed up program development and ensures that a defined subclass is inherently valid.

initialization *v*. The process of locating and using the defined values for variable data that is used by a computer program. For example, when an operating system starts up, it seeks initialization files to provide values that can be substituted (files that end with '.ini' are considered initialization files).

inoperability *v*. The inability of hardware and software applications to work together. Many software companies are developing their own communication standards (e.g. Biztalk, ebXML) which makes it difficult for applications to work together properly without mass customization.

input/output (I/O) *n*. Any operation, program, or device that transfers data to or from a computer. Common I/O devices include printers, hard disks, keyboards, and mouse's.

instantiate *v*. An object-oriented programming term; to create such an instance by, for example, defining one particular variation of object within a class, giving it a name, and locating it in some physical place.

Integrated Services Digital Network (ISDN) *n*. Basically a way to move more data over existing regular phone lines. It can provide speeds

---

of 64,000 bits-per-second over a regular phone line at almost the same cost as a normal phone call.

integration *n.* The combining of parts so that they work together or form a whole system. Often it's the process of bringing different manufacturers' products together into a smoothly working system.

intelligent agent *n.* An internet program that gathers information or performs some other service without your immediate presence and on some regular schedule. For example, there are intelligent agents that search all or part of the internet, gather information that you're interested in, and present it to you on a daily or other periodic basis. An agent is sometimes called a bot or robot.

interchange *n.* EDI communication between trading partners in the form of a structured set of messages and service data segments starting with an interchange control header and ending with an interchange control trailer.

interchange agreement *n.* An agreement that lays down the conditions and obligations of partners exchanging information by EDI.

interchange control *n.* A layer around an electronic envelope in an EDI document that contains information regarding the control numbers, send and receiver ID's, and other relevant information.

interconnect *n.* The transmission of EDI documents from one VAN (See Value Added Network) to another.

interested party *n.* A prime contractor or an actual or perspective offeror whose direct economic interest would be affected by the award of a contract or by the failure to award a contract.

interface 1. *v.* A programming interface, consisting of a set of statements, functions, and other ways of expressing program instructions and data provided by a program or language for a programmer to use. 2. *v.* A user interface, consisting of operating system commands, graphical display formats, and other devices provided by a computer or a program to allow the user to communicate and use the computer or program.

interlaced GIF *n.* A graphic image that gradually comes into focus on your computer screen when being downloaded on the World Wide Web. These types of images are important to users who have slow connections who may have enough information about the image to make a decision to click on it or move elsewhere.

International Accounting Standards (IAS) *n.* Accounting standards issued by the International Accounting Standards committee. Some of the advantages claimed for international standards are that financial statements prepared in different countries will be more comparable, multinational companies will find preparation of accounts easier, and listing on different stock exchanges can be achieved more simply. However, international standards are not mandatory.

International Standards Organization (ISO) *n.* A worldwide federation of national standards bodies from various countries. Its mission is to promote the development of standards to facilitate the international exchange of goods and services, and develop cooperation in intellectual, scientific, technological and economic activity. Also known as the International Organization for Standardization.

International Telecommunications Union (ITU) *n.* The specialized telecommunications agency of the United Nations, established to provide standardized communication procedures and practices. Formerly CCITT.

internet *n.* The series of interconnected networks that includes local area, regional, and national backbone networks. Networks in the Internet use the same telecommunications protocol (TCP/IP) and provide electronic mail, remote login, and file transfer services. See also Telnet, File Transfer Protocol, browser, World Wide Web.

Internet Architecture Board (IAB) *n.* An internet organization of scientists and engineers that supervises the Internet Engineering Task Force (IETF), which oversees the evolution of TCP/IP, and the Internet Assigned Numbers Authority (IANA) which oversees the allocation of IP numbers. They're located on the web at http://www.iab.org.

Internet Engineering Task Force (IETF) *n.* An organization that defines the standard internet operating protocol TCP/IP and directs its development.

Internet Information Server (IIS) *n.* A group of internet servers that run on the Window's NT and Window's 2000 operating systems developed by Microsoft. Components of the Internet Information Server include an HTTP server, FTP server, Active Server Page (ASP) technology, ISAPI application program interface for programmers to add capabilities, and ActiveX controls which can be embedded in web pages (similar to a Java applet).

Internet Message Access Protocol (IMAP) *n.* A standard protocol for accessing email from a mail server. Perhaps the most attractive quality of IMAP is the ability to retrieve mail from your server, yet a copy of your mail is still held on the server. IMAP is a protocol generally used by users who may access their mail from many different computers. POP3 is a similar protocol, however when you download a message it is erased on the server; the only copy of your mail message is on your local machine.

Internet Protocol (IP) *n.* The Internet standard protocol that provides a common layer over dissimilar networks, used to move packets among host computers and through gateways if necessary. See also TCP/IP.

Internet Relay Chat (IRC) *n.* A protocol used on the Internet that allows people to engage in chat sessions between each other using a text based user interface.

Internet Service Provider (ISP) *n.* An organization that provides access to the Internet and other services such as electronic mail accounts and data storage.

InterNIC *n.* The Internet Network Information Center, a cooperative activity between the U.S. government and Network Solutions, Inc., was the organization responsible for registering and maintaining top-level domains (.com, .net, and .org). This responsibility has been distributed to many other companies in 2000.

interoperability *adj.* The ability of a system or product to work with other systems or products without added customization on the part of the customer. By adhering to published interface standards, vendor products have been able to "claim" that their products are completely interoperable, however this isn't always the case (standards aren't always completely followed).

interpreter *n.* A computer program that executes a program written in a programming language without first translating it into machine code; for example when Java code is executed on a platform, it uses an interpreter.

interrupt *n.* A signal from a device attached to a computer or from a program within the computer that causes the operating system to stop and figure out what to do next. An operating system usually has some code called an interrupt handler that prioritizes the interrupts and saves them in a queue if more than one is waiting to be handled.

intrinsic value *adj.* The value something has because of its nature, before it has been processed in any way.

inventory *n.* Quantity on hand for an item in a catalog.

inventory inquiry/advice *n.* The 846 document of the ANSI X12 EDI transaction sets (see appendix). A request for the availability information of a particular product.

inverse multiplexing *n.* A process for speeding up data transmission by dividing a data stream into multiple concurrent streams that are transmitted at the same time across separate channels and are then reconstructed at the other end into the original data stream.

invitation for bid *n.* Solicitation document used in sealed bidding and in the second step of two step sealed bidding.

invoice *n.* A list of goods or services sent to a purchaser showing information including prices, quantities and shipping charges for payment.

IP *n.* See Internet Protocol (IP).

IP address *n.* The numeric address of a computer connected to the Internet; also called an Internet address. This is a unique number on the internet with the exception of your local machine that is always 127.0.0.1. IP Address's are split into four different segments and can be compared to a telephone number. However, instead of typing a 4 segment number into your browser address field, it's easier to type and remember a alphanumeric string like "rockbend.com" instead of "63.45.23.127". See also Domain Name System (DNS).

IRA *n.* Abbreviation for individual retirement account.

IRC *n*. See Internet Relay Chat (IRC).

ISAPI *n*. An acronym for Internet Server Application Program Interface; a set of Windows program calls that allow a programmer to write a web server application that will run faster than a CGI (common gateway interface) application on the IIS (Internet Information Server) platform.

ISDN *n*. See Integrated Services Digital Network (ISDN).

ISO *n*. See International Standards Organization (ISO).

ISO 9000 *n*. A set of standards, developed and published by the International Standards Organization (ISO), that define a quality system for manufacturing and service industries. An organization can be ISO 9000-certified if it successfully follows the ISO 9000 standards for its industry. An outside assessor performs an examination of the organization to determine certification.

ISO 14000 *n*. A series of environmental management standards developed and published by the International Standards Organization (ISO) for organizations. It provides a framework for organizations that need to systemize and improve their environmental management efforts.

ISO date format *n*. The International Organization for Standardization date format is a standard way to express a calendar date that eliminates cross-country confusion. For example, British citizens usually write the date before the month (e.g. 04-07-1776). The separators used between numbers also vary between countries. The ISO approach dictates that year should be first, followed by month, then day, separated by a hyphen ("-"). For example, July 4, 1776 would be expressed as: 1776-07-04.

isochronous *n*. The processes that require timing coordination to be successful, such as voice and digital video transmission. Isochronous can be distinguished from asynchronous, which refers to processes that proceed independently of each other until a dependent process has to "interrupt" the other process, and synchronous, which refers to processes in which one process has to wait on the completion of an event in another process before continuing.

ISP *n.* See Internet Service Provider (ISP).

IT *n.* See Information Technology (IT).

iterative *n.* In a software implementation environment, iterative is used to describe a planning and development process where an application or system is developed in small sections called iterations. Each iteration is reviewed and evaluated by the implementation team and potential end-users; insights gained from the evaluation of an iteration are used to determine the next step in development. The ultimate challenge of operating in this manner is ensuring that all iterations are compatible and interoperable with previously completed sections.

ITU *n.* See International Telecommunications Union (ITU).

Jj

J2EE *n.* An acronym for Java 2 Platform, Enterprise Edition; a Java platform designed for mainframe-scale computing typical of large information technology centers. Sun Microsystems designed J2EE to simplify application development in a thin-client tiered environment.

JAR file *n.* A Java Archive file; a file that contains the class, image, and sound files for a Java applet gather into a single file and compression for faster downloading to your web browser. A Jar file is specified similar to this in a web page's Hypertext Markup Language (HTML):

```
<applet code=helloWorld.class archive=hello.jar width=200
height=200>
</applet>
```

Java *n.* A programming language introduced by Sun Microsystems in 1995; it's expressly designed for use in a distributed environment of the Internet. It was modeled against the C++ language, but was meant to be simpler and enforces an object-oriented programming model. Java can be used to create applications that run on a single computer or be distributed among servers and clients in a network.

Java Database Connectivity (JDBC) *n.* An application program interface specification for connecting programs written in Java to

---

databases (such as Oracle, and MSsql). The application program interface allows code access request statements in SQL (structured query language) that are then passed to the program that manages the database. JDBC is similar to the SQL Access Group's Open Database Connectivity (ODBC) interface.

Java Server Page (JSP) *n.* A technology for controlling the content or appearance of Web pages through the use of a servlet, programs that are marked up in a web page and run on the web server to modify the page before it is sent to the user who requested it. JSP is comparable to Microsoft's Active Server Page (ASP) technology. Some web pages that have the suffix '.jsp' will contain a link to a Java servlet.

Javabeans *n.* An object-oriented programming interface developed by Sun Microsystems that allows you to build re-usable program building blocks called components that can be deployed in a network or any major operating system platform. To build a component with JavaBeans, you write language statements using Sun's Java programming language and include statements that describe component properties such as events that trigger a bean to communicate with beans in the same container or elsewhere in the network. Due to the modularity, JavaBeans are easily modified and transportable across the network.

Javascript *n.* A script language originally developed by Netscape engineer Brenden Eich for use on the World Wide Web. Javascript uses some of the same ideas found in Java, but is considerably less complicated and easier to use. Both Microsoft and Netscape browsers support Javascript, however they've implemented the standard in different ways.

Java Foundation Classes (JFC) *n.* Pre-written code in the form of class libraries that gives the developer a set of graphical user interface routines to use. JFC is an extension of the original Java Abstract

Windowing Toolkit (AWT). Using JFC and Swing, a programmer can write programs that are independent of the operating system within a particular environment.

Java Message Service (JMS) *n.* A standards-based messaging service based on the Java programming language. This type of technology allows software applications to send data back and forth; essentially this is a way for computers to talk to one another and exchange data, such as purchase orders.

JHTML *n.* A file or web page containing Java programming code; the code in a JHTML web page is interpreted on-the-fly into a small program that is executed at the server before the web page is sent to the user. Web pages that use this technology will usually have the extension '.jhtml'.

JINI *n.* Developed by Sun Microsystems (pronounced gee-nee), it's the ability to plug in any device on the network and every other computer, device, and user on the network will know that the new device has been added and is available. JINI promises to enable manufacturers to make devices that can attach to a network independently of an operating system like Windows.

JIT *n.* See Just In Time (JIT).

JMS *n.* See Java Message Service (JIT).

job 1. *n.* An identifiable discrete piece of work carried out by an organization. For costing purposes, a job is usually given a job number. 2. *n.* A process waiting to be executed on a computer, usually a mainframe.

job satisfaction *n.* The sense of fulfillment and pride felt by people who enjoy their work and do it well. This feeling is enhanced if the significance of the work done and its value are recognized by those in authority.

joint venture *n*. The temporary association of two or more businesses to secure and fulfill a procurement bid award.

JPEG *n*. A graphic image created by choosing from a range of picture qualities called a compression algorithm. When creating a JPEG, the user is presented with the option to create a low-quality image (minimum file size) or the highest quality image (maximum file size). JPEG is an acronym for Joint Photographic Experts Group, the organization that established the original algorithms. JPEG is one of the image file formats supported on the World Wide Web, usually with the file suffix of '.jpg'.

Jscript *n*. A script language developed by Microsoft that designed for use within web pages. It adheres to the ECMAScript standard and is Microsoft's answer to Netscape's more widely used Javascript implementation.

Just In Time (JIT) *n*. 1. The concept of reducing inventories by working closely with suppliers to coordinate deliveries of materials, or parts, just before their use in the manufacturing or assembly process. 2. Just In Time compilers; computer code which is compiled only when a request is made.

Kk

KB *n*. See Kilobyte (KB).

KBPS *n*. Kilobits per second (thousands of bits per second); a measure of bandwidth on a data transmission medium. Due to rising bandwidth capabilities, KBPS is a term rarely used (MBPS and GBPS are the higher rates).

keep it simple, stupid (KISS principle) *n*. The result of over-thinking and too many people involved in one project sometimes turns simple ideas into over-complicated and confusing plans. Developers and managers sometimes need to be reminded of the KISS principle.

kerberos *n*. A secure method for authenticating a request for a service in a computer network. Kerberos lets a user request an encrypted key from an authentication process that can then be used to request a particular service from a server. The user's password does not have to pass through the network. It was originally developed at MIT and can be downloaded at http://web.mit.edu/www/kerberos.

kernel *n*. The core of a computer system that provides basic services for all other parts of the operating system.

KHZ *n*. A kilohertz is a unit of alternating current or electromagnetic

---

wave currency equal to one thousand hertz. The unit is also used in measurements or statements of signal bandwidth.

kickback *n.* Any money, fee, commission, credit, gift, gratuity, thing of value, or compensation of any kind which is provided, directly or indirectly, to agency procurement or program officials by any prime contractor employee, subcontractor, or subcontractor employee for the purpose of improperly obtaining or receiving favorable treatment in connection with obtaining a contract. It's common for upper management to receive kickbacks from e-business consulting companies and vendors seeking fees.

killer app *n.* A term in the computer industry for an application that intentionally or unintentionally gets you to make the decision to buy it. Examples of killer app's include Lotus 1-2-3, Microsoft Office, and Netscape's browser application. These applications introduced new technologies that eventually became mainstream.

kilobyte (KB) *n.* A thousand bytes (actually 1024 bytes).

kilocharacter *n.* 1000 characters; a unit of measure for tracking and reporting traffic volume on VANs and exchanges. Generally, VAN's will base their pricing on number of kilocharacters transmitted by a customer.

Kip *n.* The standard monetary unit of Laos.

kludge *n.* (pronounced klooj) An awkward, temporary solution to a programming or application implementation problem. A kludge is often a replacement for an effective solution that cannot be implemented due to time constraints.

knowledge management *n.* The name of a concept in which an organization consciously and comprehensively gathers, organizes, shares, and analyzes its acquired knowledge in terms of resources, documents, and people skills. Knowledge management involves data mining and some method to make the data available to users. The biggest challenge in knowledge management systems is encouraging employees to use and contribute to the enterprise system.

knowledge worker *n.* Anyone who works for a living at the tasks of developing or using knowledge. A knowledge worker might be someone who works at any of the tasks of planning, acquiring, searching, analyzing, organizing, or otherwise contributing to the transformation and commerce of information. Programmers, technical writers, researchers, etc. are examples of knowledge workers.

korn shell *n.* A UNIX shell or command interpreter developed by David Korn of Bell Labs as a combined version of other major UNIX shells (C shell, Bourne shell). The default character displayed to indicate readiness for user input is the '$' sign.

Koruna *n.* The standard monetary unit of the Czech Republic and Slovakia.

Krona *n.* The standard monetary unit of Sweden.

Krone *n.* The standard monetary unit of Denmark, the Faroe Islands, Greenland, and Norway.

Ll

last-in-first-out (LIFO) *n.* A strategy for order fulfillment or criteria for logic to execute. Simply put, the last order that was received is the first one to be sent out.

late bid *n.* Any bid or proposal received after the designated date and time listed on the solicitation.

latency *n.* Usually refers to a delay of some type, its an expression of how much time it takes for a packet of data to get from one designated point to another. Latency assumes that data should be transmitted instantly between one point to another.

laying off *v.* Suspending or terminating the employment of workers because of lack of work or replaced by a new piece of technology (e.g. E-Business).

LDAP *n.* See Lightweight Directory Access Protocol (LDAP).

LDAP Data Interchange Format (LDIF) *n.* The main file format used to import or export data from an LDAP directory or database. LDIF files are ASCII text files that represent data in a format that is recognizable to an LDAP directory, or database. Below is an example of an LDIF.

```
dn: o=Rockbend, c=US
objectclass: organization
o: Rockbend
aci: (target ="ldap:///o=Rockbend, c=US")(targetattr
!="userPassword")(version 3.0;acl "anonymous
  access";allow (read, search, compare)(userdn = "ldap:///anyone");)
aci: (target="ldap:///o=Rockbend, c = US") (targetattr =
"*")(version 3.0; acl "allow
 self write"; allow(write) userdn = "ldap:///self";)
```

The above values give definitions to the hierarchy of the LDAP directory. The directory name (dn) is Ace Industry based in the US (c). The access control values (aci) essentially allows anyone to read, search, and compare entries in the LDAP.

lead time *n.* The time that it would take a supplier to delivery goods after receipt of order.

lease *n.* A contract conveying from one entity to another the use of real or personal property for a designated period of time in return for payment or other consideration.

legacy application *n.* Applications within the enterprise that have endured many changes and continue to meet critical business needs. Generally, legacy applications are earmarked to be upgraded or converted to new technology. Theoretically, this will make it easier to update applications without considerable rewrite, and will allow them to run more smoothly.

Lek *n.* The standard monetary unit of Albania; its three character currency code is 'ALL'.

lessee *n.* One to whom a lease is granted.

lessor *n.* One who grants a lease.

leverage *n.* Any strategic or tactical advantage that will be exploited. In a business-to-business environment, organizations are leveraging existing data (data storage, data mining, and databases) to formulate new-economy business plans.

life cycle costing *n.* A procurement evaluation technique that determines the total cost of acquisition, operation, maintaining and disposal of the items acquired; the lowest ownership cost during the time the item is in use.

LIFO *n.* See last-in-first-out (LIFO).

Lightweight Directory Access Protocol (LDAP) *n.* A network protocol that extracts information from a hierarchical directory, such as a user name, e-mail address, security certificate, and other contact information. A LDAP repository has its own authentication and access control functions. LDAP is a "lightweight" version of the Directory Access Protocol (DAP), which is a part of the X.500 standard for directory services in a network. It originated at the University of Michigan and Netscape was one of the first commercial vendor's to release it publicly, aptly named Netscape Directory Server.

line item *n.* An item of supply or service specified in a solicitation for which the vendor must specify a separate price.

Linux *n.* Usually pronounced LYNN-ICKS, however some people pronounce it LYE-NICKS. The argument is amusing, sometimes neophytes use the latter term because they assume Linus Torvolds (original creator of Linux) has the American pronunciation, similar to the Peanuts character. However, in Finnish (Finland is his home country) Linus is pronounced LEE-NUS. A rose by any other name…

Linux is a free operating system and the most popular UNIX based OS available. It has a reputation as a very efficient and fast-performing system.

Linux has set off a type of revolution among computer programmers, scientists, and researchers. Corporations are beginning to become a larger part of the user-base as the operating system matures and becomes more accepted among the mainstream.

liquidated damages *n.* A specific sum of money, agreed to as part of a contract to be paid by one party to the other in the event of a breach of contract in lieu of actual damages, unless otherwise provided by law.

Lira *n.* The standard monetary unit of Italy, Turkey, and Malta.

list price *n.* The price of an article published in a catalog, advertisement or printed list from which discounts, if any, may be subtracted.

liteware *n.* A software application that has limited capabilities compared to the full "for-sale" version. It's usually designed to provide potential customers with a sample of the product to assist in their purchasing decisions. Adobe Photoshop LE is a common example of liteware where the user is unable to save files until the full version is purchased.

load balancing *n.* The process of dividing the amount of work that a computer has to do between two or more computers so that more work can be accomplished in the same amount of time and , in general, all users get served faster. Typically, an application server that is clustered will have load balancing enabled to process requests efficiently and quickly.

Local Area Network (LAN) *n.* A computer network limited to the immediate area, usually the same building or floor of the building.

locale *n.* A particular country or region that uses different settings for language, number and date formats, graphics, and page layout.

localization *n.* The process of modifying a specific application for an international market, which includes translating the graphical interface, resizing dialog boxes, customizing features, and testing results to ensure that the application works properly in the new locale. Ideally, a product or service is developed so that localization is relatively easy to achieve. See locale.

logical partition *n.* A division of a computer's processors, memory, and storage into multiple sets of resources so that each set of resources can be operated independently with the operating system and applications on it.

login 1. *n.* The account name used to gain access to a computer system. 2. *v.* The act of entering a computer system.

logistics 1. *n.* The management of material and information flows through an organization to its customers; the overall function of sourcing and distributing material and product in the proper place and in proper quantities. 2. *n.* The detailed planning of any complex operation.

logoff *v.* The procedure by which a user begins a terminal or application session.

logon *v.* The procedure by which a user ends a terminal or application session.

Lombard Street *n.* A street in the city of London that is the center of the money markets. Many commercial banks have offices in or near Lombard street.

loop *v.* A repetitive sequence of events that occur until a condition is met. For example, most programming languages have the ability to do a loop, where statements are repetitively executed until the desired outcome results.

lossless compression *n.* A term which describes whether or not, in the compression of a file, all original data can be recovered when the file is uncompressed. Every single bit of data that was originally in the file remains after the file is uncompressed.

low level *adj.* Someone who is speaking in great detail and preparation. This is the antonym of *high level*, someone who is speaking in general and non-specific terms.

ltd *n.* The usual abbreviation for limited; an organizational type.

Mm

m-commerce *n.* Mobile commerce; the buying and selling of goods and services through wireless devices such as personal digital assistants (PDA's). Much of m-commerce is based on the Wireless Application Protocol (WAP) which allows mobile devices to access the World Wide Web.

MAC *n.* See Message Authentication Coding (MAC).

MAC address *n.* Media Access Control address; a unique hardware number on computer equipment. Typically, a MAC address is used on a local area network to identify each computer.

machine code *n.* The base language of computers, consisting of a stream of 0's and 1's. When a program or application is compiled, it's translated into output that is machine code. This type of machine code can be stored as an executable file until someone decides to execute it.

machine down-time *n.* The period during which a machine cannot be used, usually because of breakdown or scheduled maintenance.

macro 1. *n.* A command in Microsoft applications that is a saved-sequence or keyboard strokes that can then be recalled with a single command. 2. *n.* Any programming or user interface that, when used, expands into something larger.

mainframe *n.* The largest type of computer, requiring an air-conditioned room and special staff, including operators, programmers, and system analysts, to run it. Used by large organizations, such as banks, they can handle vast amounts of information with ease and calculate at high speed. They can also handle many users simultaneously. IBM is a market leader in producing mainframe computers.

majordomo *n.* It's Latin root meaning "master of the house"; a small program that automatically redistributes e-mail to names on a mailing list. Majordomo is written in Perl and can be run on any operating system platform.

makefile *n.* A file used to determine which portions of a program to compile. It's basically a guide for the make utility to choose the appropriate program file that is to be compiled and linked together. A makefile contains three types of information for the make program: a target (the name of what the user is trying to construct); the rules (commands that tell how to construct the target from the sources) and a dependency. To create a makefile, make a file containing shell commands and name it 'makefile'.

managed currency *n.* A currency in which the government controls, or at least influences, the exchange rate. This control is usually exerted by the central bank buying and selling in the foreign-exchange market.

Management Information System (MIS) *n.* A system that assists management to gather and process information to enable them to make better decisions. Most modern management information systems provide the data from an integrated computer database, which is constantly updated from all areas of the organization in a structured way. Access to the data is usually restricted to the areas regarded as useful to particular managers. Access to confidential information is limited to top management. An MIS should run parallel to the configuration of the physical and organizational structure. The application of information technology has enabled MIS to drive these structures.

manifest *n.* A list of all the cargo carried by a ship, truck or aircraft. It has to be signed by the captain (or first officer) before being handed to customs on leaving and arriving at a port or airport.

manufacturing costs *n.* Items of expense incurred to carry out the manufacturing process in an organization. They include direct materials, direct labor, direct costs, and manufacturing overhead.

map *n.* The file used to translate one form of data into another. Also see Mapping.

mapping *n.* The process of identifying a standard data element's relationship to business application data (or elements within that data). The process of translating one form of data into another. Examples of mapping software include Mercator (http://www.mercator.com) and Gentran.

maquiladora *n.* Spanish for 'twin plant'; the practice of building factories that straddle the US-Mexican border, enabling US companies to take advantage of lower Mexican labor costs.

marginal cost *n.* The variable costs per unit of production. The variable costs are usually regarded as the direct costs plus the variable overheads. Marginal cost represents the additional cost incurred as a result of the production of one additional unit of production.

market price *n.* The price of a raw material, product, service, security, etc., in an open market.

Markka *n.* The standard monetary unit of Finland.

mark-up *n.* The amount by which the cost of a service or product has been increased to arrive at a selling price. It is calculated by expressing the profit as a percentage of the cost or service. For example, if a product cost $10 to produce and is sold for $15, the markup would be: $10/$15 * 100 = 50%.

marquee partners *n.* The organizations and/or customer's which provide the highest strategic value. For example, Intel and Microsoft probably consider each other marquee partners.

marshalling *v.* A computer programming term; the process of gathering data from one or more application or non-contiguous sources in computer storage, putting the data pieces into a message buffer, and organizing or converting the data into a format that is prescribed for a particular receiver or programming interface. Marshalling is usually required when passing the output parameters of a program written in one language as input to a program written in another language.

materials management *n.* Embraces all functions of acquisition, standards, quality control and surplus property management; management of the flows of materials through an organization's immediate supply chain which specifically includes purchasing, inventory management, operations planning and control, distribution to customers, and the management of information flows. Effectively, for every unit of material flow in one direction through the supply chain, there is an equivalent information flow in the opposite direction. Information technology has improved the efficiency in information flow.

material release *n.* The document which completes a blanket purchase order. Procurement departments will send blanket purchase orders to establish minimum parameters such as a range for quanity and price. Demand dictates how many parts will be ordered from the supplier, which is done by sending a material release. It's also referred to as an 830, the ANSI X12 Transaction Set number.

Material Requirements Planning (MRP) *n.* A production schedule which organizes the placement of materials where and when they are required. Also known as Materials Planning.

maverick purchasing *v.* The purchasing practice of individuals or entire departments where they buy "off-contract" without taking advantage of a pre-negotiated rate with a competing supplier. These type of purchases are usually done with a corporate credit card where convenience, speed, and laziness are the attributing factors to the final purchasing decision.

maximum order limitation *n.* Dollar limits of any single delivery order by item and by total order.

MB *n.* See Megabyte (MB).

mbps *n.* Millions of bits per second or megabits per second; a measure of bandwidth on a telecommunications line.

megabyte (MB) *n.* A million bytes. A thousand kilobytes.

megahertz *n.* A million cycles of electromagnetic currency alternation per second and is used as a unit of measure for a computer microprocessors clock speed.

memory *n.* The storage section of a computer in which data and programs are held.

memory leak *n.* The gradual loss of available computer memory when a program or application repeatedly fails to return memory that it has obtained for temporary use. Available memory for that application or that part of the operating system becomes exhausted and the program can no longer function. Programs that run continuously (e.g. server

programs like web servers) with very small memory leaks can
eventually cause the program to terminate. This is a very common
problem among all software applications and operating systems due to
the pressure felt from a rapid application development environment.

menu *n.* A list of choices displayed by a computer and the applications
running on it. When many options are available, the user may first be
presented with a main menu from which more detailed menus can be
selected. A well-designed menu system can make a complex program
simple to use.

Message Authentication Coding (MAC) *n.* A cryptographically
derived hash total used to verify the authorized sender to the authorized
receiver and protect the integrity of the data.

Message Transfer Agent (MTA) *n.* A component of an X.400
network that transmits electronic messages to local users and forwards
messages on to other MTAs.

meta character *n.* A special character in a program or data field that
provides information about other characters. For example, a backslash
(\) is used to indicate the beginning of a line for comments in many
programming languages.

metadata *n.* A definition or description of data. The Extensible
Markup Language (XML) is a describing language, and an XML file
could be considered completely full with metadata.

metafile *n.* A file containing information that describes or specifies
another file. An example of a metafile is the Computer Graphics
Metafile (CGM). The CGM file format is a standard format that can be
used on any operating system that supports and is commonly used in
CAD and presentation graphics applications.

method *n.* A procedure in object-oriented programming that is defined as part of a class and included in any object of that class. A method in an object can only have access to the data known to that object, which ensures data integrity among the set of objects in an application.

metric *n.* A standard of measurement for performance. Performance reports are comprised of many different metrics.

middleman *n.* A person or organization that makes a profit by trading in goods as an intermediary between the producer and consumer. Middlemen include agents, brokers, dealers, merchants, factories, wholesalers, distributors, and retailers. They earn their profit by providing a variety of different services, including finance, bulk buying, holding stocks, breaking bulk, risk sharing, making a market and stabilizing prices, providing information about products to consumers and providing information about markets to producers. It also provides a distribution network, and introduces buyers to sellers.

middleware *n.* A term used in a distributed computing environment; part of the system architecture that executes heavy-processing logic; e.g. application servers. In an application diagram, this piece of software would reside somewhere in the "middle".

migration *n.* Method for moving previous versions of data to another application, usually an updated version.

MIME *n.* See Multipurpose Internet Mail Extensions (MIME).

MIS *n.* See Management Information System (MIS).

modification of bid *n.* A bidder may modify their bid only if the modification is received in the bid opening office prior to the time set for opening the bids.

monetary unit *n.* The standard unit of currency in a country. The monetary unit of each country is related to those of other countries by a foreign exchange rate.

monopsony *n.* A market in which there is only a single buyer.

Moore's law *n.* Gordon E. Moore, one of the founder's of Intel, said in 1965 that the processing power of integrated circuits would double every 18 months for the next 10 years. This law has been proven generally true for over 30 years and is now used in many application performance forecasts. Some people debate that 18 months isn't true, that it's more like 24 months. Moore's second law is that the cost of production would double every generation.

moratorium *n.* An act authorizing postponement of payments; a delay.

Mozilla *n.* Originally a Netscape Communications nickname for the Navigator web browser. Mozilla is now the name for an open source effort to build a standards-based web browser. Mozilla is also the name of a mascot and cartoon alter ego created by illustrator Dave Titus.

MRO *n.* Abbreviation for Maintenance and Repair Organization. Term also commonly used to refer to low-dollar, high volume transactions.

MS-DOS *n.* Abbreviation for Microsoft disk operating system. This disk operating system for personal computers is produced by the corporation Microsoft; designed originally for the IBM personal computer, it is found on most Microsoft platforms.

MTA *n.* See Message Transfer Agent.

multi-currency *n.* A feature that allows for multiple currencies within one system or within one requisition.

multi-locale *n.* A feature that allows for multiple locales to be in use within one application or system.

multi-org *n.* A feature that allows multiple unique entities within an application. This allows organizations to have their own private locations, suppliers, contracts, catalogs, etc.

multicast *n.* A communication process between a single sender and multiple receivers on a network. System administrators may send out a multicast message when there is scheduled maintenance on a system.

multiple-unit pricing *n.* Selling more than one unit of a product at a lower price than twice the unit price. 'Buy three, get one free' is an example.

multiple award *n.* Contracts awarded to more than one supplier for comparable supplies and services. Awards are made for the same generic types of items at various prices.

Multipurpose Internet Mail Extensions (MIME) *n.* A protocol that allows binary files to be attached to electronic mail messages. The files are converted to text and sent, and then converted back to their original state by the recipient's mail software.

multitasking 1. *adj.* Describing a computer system that can run more than one program at the same time. 2. *v.* A person performing more than one task at a single moment of time (e.g. walking and chewing gum).

multithreading *v.* The ability of a program or process to manage its use by more than one user at a time and to even manage multiple requests by the same user without having to have multiple copies of the program running in the computer.

MySAP *n.* An e-business application made by the German software company SAP. Its functionality covers customer relationship management (CRM), supply-chain management, e-procurement, business intelligence, product lifecycle management, human resources, and financial and marketplace channels. Users access the application

with a web browser through their mySAP Web portal, called
"Workplace". Access to the mySAP.com Workplace portal is based on a
per-user or per-number-of-transactions fee model.

Nn

Naira *n.* The standard monetary unit of Nigeria.

namespace *n.* A component of the Extensible Markup Language (XML) specification. A namespace is a document at one specific web site that identifies the names of particular data elements or attributes used within the XML file.

natural wastage *n.* The method by which an organization can contract without making people redundant, relying on resignations, retirements, or deaths. If the time is available, this method of reducing a workforce causes the least tension.

NAPM *n.* See National Association of Purchasing Management (NAPM).

National Association of Purchasing Management (NAPM) *n.* National Association of Purchasing Management. A nonprofit educational and technical organization of purchasing and materials management personnel and buying agencies from the public and private sectors.

NDA *n.* See non-disclosure agreement (NDA).

NDS *n*. See Novell Directory Services (NDS).

negative cash flow *n*. A cash flow in which the outflows exceed the inflows.

negotiation *n*. Requests for proposals are sometimes used as a starting point for negotiations to establish a contract. RFPs generally include more than just price considerations. This method is especially applicable when dealing with a single source manufacturer.

net *n*. Denoting an amount remaining after specific deductions have been made. For example, net profit before taxes is the profit made by an organization after the deduction of all business expenses but before the deduction of taxes.

net margin *n*. The gross margin less all the other costs of an organization in addition to those included in the cost of goods sold.

net price *n*. Price of a purchase order after discounts and charges have been applied.

Netscape *n*. A corporation that produces a common web browser for the World Wide Web, now a subsidiary of AOL Time Warner. Netscape invented and refined many of the core technologies used on the web today including secure-sockets layer (ssl), Javascript, Frames, and other commerce technologies.

Netscape Server Application Programming Interface (NSAPI) *n*. An application program interface that is provided with Netscape's server programs that helps developers build more complex web applications by extending the server capabilities.

netting *v*. The process of setting off matching sales and purchases against each other, especially sales and purchases of futures and options in an exchange.

---

network *n.* A linked set of computer systems, terminals, servers, and peripherals capable of sharing computer power or storage facilities.

Network File System (NFS) *n.* A client/server application that lets a user view and optionally store and update files on a remote computer as though they were on the user's own computer. The user or system administrator can mount all or a portion of a file system, which can be accessed with whatever privileges go with your access to each file (read-only, read-write-execute, etc.). NFS was developed by Sun Microsystems and is very popular application on all UNIX-based operating systems.

new entrants *n.* Organizations entering an industry for the first time. They may be new organizations or established organizations entering a new field.

New Sol *n.* The standard monetary unit of Peru.

news release *n.* A brief written statement sent to the press describing a company's new product, product improvement, price change, or some other development of interest. The release will only be published if it is sufficiently newsworthy.

next-in-first-out cost (NIFO) *n.* A method of valuing units of raw material or finished goods issued from stock by using the next unit price at which a consignment will be received for pricing units.

NFS *n.* See Network File System (NFS).

Ngultrum *n.* The standard monetary unit of Bhutan.

no bid *n.* A response to a solicitation for bids stating that respondent does not wish to submit an offer. It usually operates as a procedure consideration to prevent suspension from the vendor's list for failure to submit a response.

nominal value *n.* A minimal price fixed for the sake of having some consideration for a transaction. It need bear no relation to the market value of the item.

non-adopter *n.* A member of a group of organizations who never buys a particular new product or adopts a certain new idea. For example, organizations that didn't join industry exchanges during the late 1990's, early 2000.

non-breaking space *n.* A special character string ( ) used in the Hypertext Markup Language (HTML) code to represent a blank space. When you type several spaces into an HTML file, only the first space is recognized; all spaces that follow are ignored. But you can use the " " character string for each blank space that you want to appear on the page.

Non-Disclosure Agreement (NDA) *n.* A signed formal agreement in which one party agrees to give a second party confidential information about its business and the second party agrees not to share this information with anyone else for a specified period of time.

non-price competition *n.* A form of competition in which two or more producers sell goods or services at the same price but compete to increase their share of the market by such measures as advertising, sales promotion campaigns, improving the quality of the product or service, delivery time, improving the packaging, installation or giving free gifts of unrelated products or services.

non-repudiation *n.* The inability of one entity involved in a communication to deny having participated in all or part of the communication.

Novell Directory Services (NDS) *n.* A software application for managing resources across a network. Using NDS, an administrator can set up and control a database of users and manage them using a directory with an easy-to-use graphical user interface. Users at remote locations can be added, updated, and managed centrally. Competing applications include Microsoft's Active Directory, and iPlanet's Directory Server (formerly Netscape's Directory Server).

NSAPI *n.* See Netscape Server Application Programming Interface (NSAPI).

Oo

OAG *n*. Acronym for Open Applications Group; a leader in standardizing common xml messaging formats for E-Business.

OASIS *n*. Organization for Structured Information Standards is a nonprofit, international consortium whose goal is to promote the adoption of product-independent standards for information formats such as the Extensible Markup Language (XML), and Hypertext Markup Language (HTML). The goal of OASIS is to provide a forum for discussion about standards, to promote the adoption of interoperability standards, and to recommend ways members can provide better interoperability for their users. Some of their current projects include sponsorship of xml.org, and ebXML.

OBI *n*. See Open Buying on the Internet (OBI).

object *n*. A term in object-oriented programming; objects are things you think about first in designing a program and they are also the units of code that are eventually derived from the process. Each object is an instance of a particular class or subclass with the class's own methods or procedures and data variables. An object is essentially what runs in the computer.

Object Management Group (OMG) *n*. An organization formed in

1989 by a group of vendors for the purpose of creating a standard architecture for distributed objects in networks. The architecture that resulted is the Common Object Request Broker Architecture (CORBA).

Object Request Broker (ORB) *n.* In a CORBA environment, an Object Request Broker (ORB) is the application that acts as a middleman between the client request for a service from a component and the completion of that request. Having an ORB running on a network means that a client program can request a service without having to understand where the server is in a distributed network or exactly what the interface to the server program looks like. An ORB can also provide security and time services.

object-oriented programming *n.* A concept organized around "objects" rather than "actions," data rather than logic. Historically, a program is viewed as a logical procedure that takes input data, processes it, and produces output data. Object-oriented programming takes the view that what we really care about are the objects we want to manipulate rather than the logic required to manipulate them. Data modeling is the first step to identify all of the objects you want to manipulate and how they relate to each other.

obsolescence *n.* A fall in the value of an asset as a result of its age. For example, plant and equipment may not have actually worn out but may have become out of date because technology has advanced and a more efficient plant or machine has become available.

Ockham's Razor *n.* Ockham's Razor is the principle proposed by William of Ockham in the fourteenth century: ``Pluralitas non est ponenda sine neccesitate'', which translates as ``entities should not be multiplied unnecessarily''. An idea that the simplest and minimal explanation is generally the correct explanation. Ockham's razor is similar to the KISS principle (keep it simple, stupid). A related rule, which can be used to slice open conspiracy theories, is Hanlon's Razor: ``Never attribute to malice that which can be adequately explained by stupidity".

octet *n.* A group of eight bits, often synonymous with byte.

OCR *n.* See Optical Character Recognition.

ODBC *n.* See Open Database Connection.

odd-even pricing *v.* The pricing of a product so that the price ends in an odd number of pennies, which is not far below the next number of dollars. For example, $19.99 might be used in preference to $20.00 in order to make the product appear cheaper.

OEM *n.* Original equipment manufacturer.

off-catalog item *n.* An item on a requisition that is described because the particular goods or services are not available from an existing catalog; the specific SKU or Product Code may not be listed.

offer *n.* A response to a solicitation that, if accepted, would bind the offeror to fulfill the resulting contract. Responses to invitations for bids (IFB) are called bids or sealed bids; responses to requests for proposals (RFP) are referred to as offers or proposals; responses to requests for quotations (RFQ) are designated as quotes.

official rate *n.* The rate of exchange given to a currency by a government. If the official rate differs from the market rate, the government has to be prepared to support its official rate by buying or selling in the open market to make the two rates coincide.

offline *adj.* Denoting computer equipment or applications that is not usable, either because it is not connected or because the system has been forbidden to use it.

offshore company *n.* A company not registered in the same country

---

as that in which the persons investing in the company are resident. For example, many US technology-consulting companies are starting organizations in India and Ireland because of the surplus of technology-savvy workers.

oligopoly *n.* A market in which relatively few sellers supply many buyers. Each seller recognizes that prices can be controlled to a certain extent and that competitors' actions will influence profits.

OMR *n.* See Optical Mark Recognition.

on approval *n.* The practice of allowing potential buyers to take possession of goods in order to decide whether or not they wish to buy them.

on order *n.* The amount of goods that has yet to arrive at a location or retail store. This includes all open purchase orders including, but not limited to, orders in transit, orders being picked, and orders being processed through customer service.

oncost *n.* The additional costs incurred as a consequence of employing personnel, or the additional costs incurred by storing and handling direct materials.

online *n.* Denoting computer equipment and applications that is connected and is usable.

online trading community *n.* See buying portal.

online transaction processing (OLTP) *n.* A program that facilitates and manages transaction-oriented applications, typically for data entry and retrieval transactions in a number of industries.

OPEC *n.* Abbreviation for Organization of the Petroleum Exporting Countries.

Open Buying on the Internet (OBI) *n.* A standards-based specification on how to purchase goods and services over the internet. It's purpose is to provide a standard framework for secure and interoperable business-to-business commerce with a focus on automating high-volume, low-dollar transactions between trading partners. The OBI architecture consists of four objects: the requisitioner, selling organization, buying organization, and payment authority.

For example, a requisitioner at a buying organization uses a web browser to select products from a catalog located at the selling organization. When the order is placed, the selling organization transmits a order request to the buyer organization for approval. The buying organization approves the order throw a pre-determined workflow process and resubmits the completed order to the selling organization.

Open Database Connectivity (ODBC) *n.* An open standard application programming interface for accessing a database. ODBC is based on and closely aligned with The Open Group standard Structured Query Language (SQL) Call-Level Interface. It allows programs to use SQL requests that will access databases without having to know the proprietary interfaces to the databases. ODBC handles the SQL request and converts it into a request the individual database system understands.

open indent *n.* An order to an overseas purchasing agent to buy certain goods, without specifying the manufacturer. If the manufacturer is specified this is a closed indent.

open-pricing agreement *n.* An agreement between firms operating in an oligopolistic market in which prices and intended price changes are circulated to those taking part in the agreement in order to avoid a price war.

Opera *n.* A compact web browser with many of the same capabilities as the two more popular browsers, Netscape's Navigator and Microsoft's Internet Explorer. Opera began in 1994 as a research project for the national phone company in Norway and is considered the third most popular browser.

Operating Resource Management (ORM) *n.* The everyday purchase of ordinary office products and services such as office supplies, furniture, computers, and travel requirements. Sometimes the term "White Collar ORM" is used as well, referring to the tools a white-collar office worker might use (paper and pen).

operating risk *n.* The inherent risk that a plant, once started, will not continue to produce at levels achieved to meet the completion definition.

operating system (OS) *n.* The software that runs a computer; e.g. Window's, Solaris, Linux. Applications software runs on top of the operating system, and is usually specific to an operating system. In larger multitasking systems, the operating system always retains control of the machine, ensuring that the separate programs do not interfere with each other and controlling the amount of processing time each receives.

Optical Character Recognition (OCR) *n.* The machine identification of printed characters. Commonly used with scanning devices to capture printed characters into the computer system.

Optical Mark Recognition (OMR) *n.* A process making use of scanning technology to read marks on a page. Commonly used on tests where multiple choice answers are required.

option *n.* A clause contained in a contract which gives an agency the unilateral right to extend the term of the contract or obtain additional quantities of products or services at the prices contained in the contract for that option period or additional quantity of products or services.

option to extend/renew *n.* A provision (or exercise of a provision) which allows a continuance of the contract for an additional time according to permissible contractual conditions.

Oracle *n.* A market leader in relational database and information management software and was the first vendor to support the Structured Query Language (SQL). Formed in 1977, Oracle is based in Redwood Shores, California and has more than 43,000 employees worldwide.

order status inquiry *n.* The 869 document of the ANSI X12 EDI transaction sets (see appendix). A request for information regarding the status of an order.

organic organization *adj.* An organization characterized by roles that are not well defined, tasks being redefined as individuals interact; there is little reliance on authority, with control and decision making decentralized, and communication is both lateral and vertical. This type of organization is common in the software industry.

organizational buying *v.* The way in which an organization (opposed to an individual consumer) identifies, evaluates, and chooses the products it buys.

ORM *n.* See Operating Resource Management (ORM).

orphan file *n.* In a computer's file system, an orphan file is a support file that no longer serves a purpose because the parent application it is associated with has been moved or deleted.

OS *n.* See Operating System.

OS/2 *n.* An operating system developed by IBM for the personal computer.

OSHA *n.* The Occupational Safety and Health Administration. Created by the OSHA Act.

out of the box *n.* Another term meaning "off the shelf," meaning ready-made software, hardware, or package that meets a need that would otherwise require a customized development effort. Many e-procurement vendors market their products with "out of the box" functionality.

outlay cost *n.* The expense incurred as the initial cost of a project or activity.

outsourcing *v.* A business decision to rely on outside suppliers or consulting firms rather than supplying resources internally. Recently this decision may be taken in the process of downsizing when specific activities have been redefined as non-core activities. In certain instances, computer, legal, and personnel services have been outsourced.

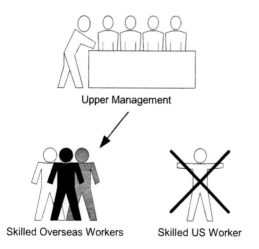

Upper Management

Skilled Overseas Workers   Skilled US Worker

outwork *n.* Work carried out in a person's own home or workshop rather than on a company's own premises.

overbought *v.* Having purchased more of a good than one needs or has orders for.

overcapacity *v.* The situation that arises when a firm or industry has greater capacity than the market demand.

oversold *v.* Having sold more of a product or service than one can produce or purchase.

Pp

P2P *n.* See peer-to-peer (P2P).

package 1. *n.* A standard unit of measure. 2. *n.* A set of computer programs designed to be sold to a number of users. Buying a software package from firms specializing in them saves users a considerable amount of time and money in developing their own. 3. *n.* A java programming term which denotes multiple java objects which is related in some fashion.

package deal *n.* An agreement that encompasses several different parts, all of which must be accepted. A package deal may have involved either or both parties in making concessions on specific aspects of the package in order to arrive at a compromise arrangement.

packet *n.* A packet is the unit of data that is routed between an origin and a destination on the Internet or any other packet-switched network. When any file is sent from one place to another on the Internet, the Transmission Control Protocol (TCP) layer of TCP/IP divides the file into "chunks" of an efficient size for routing.

packet switching *v.* In packet switching, all the data coming out of a machine is broken up into chunks, each chunk has the address of where it came from and where it is going. This enables chunks of data from many different sources to co-mingle on the same lines, and be sorted and directed to different routes by special machines along the way. This way many people can use the same lines at the same time.

packing list *n.* A document that itemizes in detail the contents of a particular package or shipment.

pallet *n.* A wooden frame on which certain goods are stacked in warehouses and during transport. Pallets are designed to be lifted by forklift trucks or pallet trucks.

paradigm *n.* A pattern or an example of something. The word also refers to the ideas of a mental picture and pattern of thought.

parallel processing *n.* A method of computing in which two or more parts of a program is executed simultaneously rather than sequentially. This usually takes place on computers with more than one central processing unit (CPU).

parameter *n.* An item of information, such as a name, that is passed to a program by a user or another program. Parameters affect the operation of the application receiving them.

parametric search *n.* Electronic search for items matching specific search parameters.

parity *n.* An equality between prices of commodities, currencies, or securities in separate markets.

par level *n.* The specified amount of inventory an enterprise wishes to have at a certain location.

par of exchange *n.* The theoretical rate of exchange between two currencies in which there is equilibrium between the supply and demand for each currency.

---

pareto rule *n.* The simplest way to describe the Pareto rule is 80/20. For example, 80% of a companies profits will generally come from 20% of the customers. If this is true, then 20% of the valued customers should receive 80% of the service. Many times however, 80% of the service goes to 20% of the bad customers.

parse *n.* To analyze something in an ordinary way. In information technology, to parse is to divide a computer language statement into parts that can be made useful for the computer or application. A parser in a program compiler is an application that takes each program statement that a developer has written and divides it into parts that can then be used for developing further actions or for creating the instructions that form an executable program.

parser *n.* In information technology, a parser is an application, usually part of a compiler, that receives input in the form of sequential source program instructions, interactive online commands, markup tags, or some other defined interface and breaks them up into parts that can then be managed by other programming. A parser may also check that all of the data is provided and that it's in a valid form.

patch *n.* A temporary repair job for a piece of an application or program. Problems (or bugs) generally result when a new piece of software is released. A patch is the immediate solution that is provided; and generally can be downloaded from the software vendor's web site. A patch is usually developed and distributed as a replacement for or an insertion in compiled code.

payee *n.* A person or organization to be paid.

payer *n.* A person or organization who makes a payment.

payment by results *n.* A system of payment in which an employee's pay is directly linked to his performance.

payment in advance *n.* Payment for goods and services before they have been received. In company accounts, this often refers to rates or rents paid for periods that carry over into the next accounting period.

payment in kind *n.* A payment that is not made in cash but in goods or services. It is often in the form of a discount or an allowance; e.g. in-store discounts for employees.

payment method *n.* The method that a customer uses to pay for a purchase order; i.e. Visa or On Account.

payment on account *n.* A payment made for goods or services before the goods or services are finally billed.

payment terms *n.* An agreement between buyer and supplier organizations on how the buyer will pay the supplier for purchases; i.e. net 30 or 2/10, 1/30.

PC *n.* Abbreviation for personal computer.

PDA *n.* Abbreviation for personal digital assistant.

Peer-to-peer (P2P) *n.* A type of internet network that allows a group of computer users with the same networking program to connect with each and directly access files from one another's hard drives. Napster and Gnutella are examples of this type of software.

pegging *n.* The fixing of the value of a country's currency on foreign exchange markets.

per diem *n.* By the day; denoting a fee charged by a professional person who is paid a specified fee for each day that he is employed.

performance bond *n.* A contract of guarantee, executed subsequent

---

to award by a successful vendor to protect the buyer from loss due to the vendor's inability to complete the contract as agreed.

performance specification *n.* A specification setting forth performance requirements determined necessary for the item involved to perform and last as required.

Perl *n.* An acronym for "Practical Extraction and Report Language," although it has also been called a "Pathologically Eclectic Rubbish Lister." Both versions have been endorsed by Larry Wall, Perl's creator and chief architect. Perl is designed to assist the programmer with common tasks that are probably too heavy or too portability-sensitive for the shell, yet too short-lived or complicated to code in C or some other UNIX shell language. Perl is distributed under the GNU Public License and versions are available for all operating systems.

perpetual inventory *n.* A method of continuous stock control in which an account is kept for each item of stock; one side of the account records the deliveries of that type of stock and the other side records the issues from the stock. This method is used in large organizations in which it is important to control the amount of capital tied up in the running of the business.

personal selling *v.* Person-to-person interaction between a buyer and a seller in which the seller's purpose is to persuade the buyer of the merits of the product, to convince the buyer of his or her need for it, and to develop with the buyer an ongoing customer relationship.

Peseta *n.* The standard monetary unit of Spain and Andorra.

Peso *n.* The standard monetary unit of Argentina, Chile, Columbia, Cuba, The Dominican Republic, Mexico, the Philippines, and Uruguay.

petabyte *n.* A measure of memory or storage capacity and is 2 to the 50th power bytes or, in decimal, approximately a thousand terabytes.

petty cash *n*. The amount of cash that an organization keeps in notes or coins on its premises to pay small items of expense.

PGP *n*. See Pretty Good Privacy (PGP).

PHP *n*. A script language and interpreter that is freely available and used primarily on Linux web servers. An earlier version of PHP was called "Personal Home Page Tools" which where the name is derived. Similar to Microsoft's Active Server Pages (ASP), a PHP script is embedded within a web page along with the HTML. When a user requests a PHP page, the web server calls PHP to interpret and perform the operation called for in the script. Like ASP, PHP can be thought of as "dynamic HTML pages," since content varies based on the results of interpreting the script.

physical distribution *n*. The tasks involved in planning, implementing, and controlling the flow of materials and final goods from their points of origin to their final destinations to meet the requirements of customers at a profit.

PIDX *n*. Petroleum Industry Data Exchange.

piece rate *n*. A payment method or scheme in which an employee is paid a specific price for each unit made in production. The rate is directly related to output and not to time.

pilot *n*. The trial run of a system or service with a closed group of selected participants. The object is to check and, if necessary, improve the production system.

ping *n*. An acronym for Packet Inter-Network Groper, ping is a program or application that lets you verify that a particular IP address exists and can accept requests. The verb ping means the act of using the ping utility or command. A common request among network

---

administrators and developers while setting up a server is "Can you ping the new e-procurement server?" thus asking to verify if the server's computer is alive on the network and can accept incoming requests. Loosely, ping means "to get the attention of" or "to check for the presence of" another machine online.

pipe *n.* A programming term on UNIX-based operating systems for passing information from one program process to another. Unlike other forms of interprocess communication, a pipe is one-way communication only. Using a UNIX shell, a pipe is specified in a command line as a simple vertical bar (|) between two command sequences. For example:

% ls *.txt | more

This command sequence performs a listing of the current directory with all files that end with the extension ".txt" and will prompt the user to continue scrolling if the result is longer than the current terminal screen. The output or result of the first command sequence (ls *.txt) was used as input to the second command sequence (more). This pipe system call is used in a similar way within a program.

Plc *n.* Abbreviation for public limited company.

PL/SQL *n.* In a database management environment, PL/SQL is a procedural language extension to the Structured Query Language (SQL) and is meant to combine database language and procedural programming. The basic unit in PL/SQL is called a block, which is made up of three parts, a declarative part, an executable part, and exception-building part. Stored Procedures are PL/SQL blocks that are stored in a database in compiled form. A PL/SQL stored procedure that implicitly started when an INSERT, UPDATE, or DELETE statement is issued against an associated table is called a trigger.

plaintext *n.* Data before it has been encrypted or after it has been decrypted, e.g. an ASCII text file.

planogram *n.* The end result of analyzing the sales data of an item or group of items to determine the best arrangement of products on a store shelf. The process determines which shelf your top-selling product should be displayed on, the number of facings it gets, and what best to surround it with. It results in graphical picture or map of the allotted shelf space along with a specification of the facing and deep.

platform *n.* An underlying computer system on which applications can run on. A platform consists of an operating system, the computer systems' coordinating program, which is built on the instruction set for a microprocessor, the hardware that performs logic operations and manages data movement in the computer. Examples of platforms include Sun Microsystems Solaris and Microsoft's Windows 2000.

PM *v.* Abbreviation for preventative maintenance.

PNG (Portable Network Graphics) *n.* A file format for image compression that is widely used on the internet. PNG is similar to the Graphics Interchange Format (GIF), but it not owned by a corporation and is patent-free. Typically, an image in a PNG file can be 10 to 30% more compressed that in a GIF format.

point of origin *n.* The location where a shipment is received by a transportation line from the shipper.

point of sale (POS) *n.* The place at which a consumer makes a purchase, usually a retail shop. Point of sale software enables the seller of a product to gather product information at the time of the sale, including the product's current price. Bar codes are often used in this process.

polymorphism *n.* An object-oriented programming term which means being able to assign different meaning to a particular symbol or operator in different contexts.

POP3 *n.* An acronym for Post Office Protocol 3, it's the most recent version of a standard protocol for receiving e-mail. POP3 is a client/server protocol in which e-mail is received and held for by your mail server. When you check your mailbox, it downloads the mail onto your local computer. A similar protocol is the Internet Message Access Protocol (IMAP), however, this protocol allows messages to be kept on the server, even if you delete your local copy. POP3 can be thought of as a "store-and-forward" service, whereas IMAP can be thought of as a remote file server.

port *n.* In information technology, a port is a logical connection place and specifically, using the Internet's protocol, TCP/IP, the way a client program specifies a particular server program on a computer in a network. Port numbers are from 0 to 65536 and 0-1024 are reserved for use by certain privileged services. For the HTTP service, port 80 is defined as a default and it does not have to be specified in the Uniform Resource Locator unless a different ports is used.

http://www.rockbend.com:22000

In this instance, the web server is on port 22000. This type of scenario is useful when a user would like two separate web servers on the same machine, thus assigning two different port numbers.

portability *n.* A characteristic attributed to a computer program if can be used in an operating system other than the one in which it was created without requiring major rework.

portal *n.* A major starting point for users when they get connected to the web or local network. Major online portals include Yahoo, Netscape, Cnet, and Google. Typical services offered by portal sites include a directory of web sites, a search facility, news, weather information, stock quotes, and sometimes community forums.

post-consumer material *n.* A finished material which would normally be disposed of as a solid waste after its life cycle as a consumer item is completed. Does not include manufacturing or converting wastes. This refers to material collected for recycling from office buildings, homes, retail stores, etc.

postscript *n.* A programming language developed by Adobe that describes the appearance of a printed page. All major printer manufacturers make printers that contain or can be loaded with Postscript software, which also runs on all major operating system platforms.

potential entrant *n.* An organization that is poised to enter a market and would do so if there was a small price rise or a reduction in barriers to entry.

Pound *n.* The standard monetary unit of Cyprus, Egypt, Lebanon, Sudan, Syria, and the United Kingdom.

powerful synergies *n.* See Synergy.

pre-approach *n.* A step in the industrial selling process in which a salesperson learns as much as possible about a prospective customer before making a sales call.

pre-consumer material *n.* Material or by-products generated after the manufacture of a product but before the product reaches the consumer, such as damaged or obsolete products. Pre-consumer material does not include mill and manufacturing trim, scrap, or broken material which is generated at a manufacturing site and commonly reused on-site in the same or another manufacturing process.

predatory pricing strategy *n.* The pricing of goods or services at such a low level that other firms cannot compete and are forced to leave the market. Many experts accused Microsoft of predatory pricing

strategy when it bundled the Internet Explorer web browser into its operating system (thus preying on Netscape).

preemptive multitasking *n.* A task in which an operating system uses some criteria to decide how long to allocate to any one task before giving another task a turn to use the operating system. The act of taking control of the operating system from one task and giving it to another task is called preempting.

pre-emption *n.* First refusal; the right of a person to be the first to be asked if he or she wishes to enter into an agreement at a specified price. For example, the right to be offered a house at a price acceptable to the vendor before it is put on the open market.

prepaid *adj.* A term denoting that transportation charges have been or is to be paid at the point of shipment.

Pretty Good Privacy (PGP) *n.* An Internet standard for securing electronic mail. It lets you encrypt a message to anyone who has a public key. You encrypt it with their public key and they then decrypt it with their private key.

preventative maintenance (PM) *n.* An approach to the maintenance of a plant, which is central to efficient techniques; it emphasizes frequent proactive inspection and repair in order to reduce downtime and to extend its working life.

price agreement *n.* A contractual agreement in which a purchaser contracts with a vendor to provide the purchaser's requirements at a predetermined price. Usually involves a minimum number of units, orders placed directly with the vendor by the purchase, and limited duration of the contract.

price analysis *n.* The process of examining and evaluating a proposed price by comparing it with other offered prices or prices previously paid

for similar goods or services.

price-bundling strategy *n.* A pricing strategy in which the price of a set of products is lower than the total of the individual prices of the components. For example, software bundling office applications is common in the software industry.

price competition *n.* A type of competition based on the price at which a product or service is offered.

price discrimination *v.* The sale of the same product at different prices to different buyers. Generally larger buyers will receive a different price than smaller buyers because of the increased levels of purchasing power.

price leadership *v.* The setting of the price of a product by a dominant firm in an industry with the knowledge that competitors will follow this lead in order to avoid the high cost of a price war.

price-lining strategy *n.* A pricing strategy in which a seller prices individual products in a product line in accordance with certain price points that are believed to be attractive to buyers.

primage *n.* An extra charge for handling goods with special care when they are being loaded or unloaded from a ship, airplane, etc.

Primary Account Number (PAN) *n.* A unique number identifying a customer for a payment system. This number is usually encrypted for security and is only visible to the customer and the acquiring bank.

prime contract *n.* A contract entered into by an agency for the purpose of obtaining supplies, materials, equipment, or services of any kind.

prime contractor *n.* A corporation, partnership, business association, trust, joint-stock company, education institution or other non-profit

organization, or individual that has entered into a prime contract with an agency.

private key *n.* One of the two keys used in an asymmetric or public key encryption system and used to exchange secret, secure messages. Only the key holder knows the private key.

procurement *n.* The combined functions of purchasing, inventory control, traffic and transportation, receiving, inspection, store keeping, and salvage and disposal operations. See e-procurement.

product adaptation *n.* The adaptation of a standard product to meet local conditions or needs, especially in foreign markets.

product obsolescence *adj.* A condition that occurs when an existing product becomes out of date as a result of the introduction of a new product or changes in taste or fashion.

proforma invoice *n.* An invoice sent in certain circumstances to a buyer, usually before some of the invoice details are known.

progressive JPEG *n.* The JPEG equivalent of an interlaced GIF. This type of image will "fade in" in successive waves of lines as its being downloaded to a users computer. Similar to the interlace GIF, a progressive JPEG is a more appealing way to deliver an image at modem connection speeds.

promiscuous mode *adj.* A mode of operation in which every data packet transmitted is received and read by every network adapter. Often used to monitor network activity, it's also used by hackers to retrieve user names, passwords, and information transmitted in data packets that are not encrypted.

promotional allowance *n.* A payment or price reduction to reward dealers for participating in advertising programs and sales-support

programs.

proprietary *n.* That which is exclusively owned by an individual or a corporation.

protest *n.* A written objection by an interested party to a procurement action conducted by an agency.

protocol *n.* A set of rules describing the transfer of data between devices. It describes the format of the data and the signals to start, control and end the transfer.

proxy server *n.* A server that acts as an intermediary between a workstation user and the internet so that the enterprise can ensure security, administrative control, and caching service. A proxy server is associated with or parts of a gateway server that separates the enterprise network from the outside network and a firewall that protects the network from outside intrusion. An advantage of a proxy server is that its cache can serve all users. If web sites are visited frequently by users in the network, it can be stored in the cache and improve user response time considerably.

public key *n.* One of the two keys used in an asymmetric or public key encryption system. The use of combined public and private keys can ensure effective encrypted messages and is known as asymmetric cryptography. The public key is widely publicized.

public key infrastructure (PKI) *n.* An infrastructure which enables users of a public network to securely and privately exchange data and money though the use of a public and private cryptographic key pair that is obtained and shared through a trusted authority.

purchase ledger *n.* The ledger in which the personal accounts of an organization's suppliers are recorded. The total of the balances in this ledger represents the organizations trade creditors.

purchase order *n.* A requisition that has been approved and sent to a supplier. This is known as an '850' order in the EDI transaction set index (see Appendix).

purchasing officer *n.* An employee of an organization, who is responsible for purchasing the raw materials used in the manufacturing process.

pure-play *adj.* A term referring to ownership in companies that focus on and specialize in a particular product or service area to the exclusion of other market opportunities in order to obtain a large market share and brand identity in one area. Examples of e-procurement organizations that are considered pure-play are Ariba and Commerce One.

push *n.* The delivery of content on the web that is initiated by the server rather than by the user or application client. This type of operation is also called a server-push.

Python *n.* An interpreted, object-orientated language similar to TCL and Perl that has gained popularity for its clear syntax and readability. Python is available on most operating systems and was created by Guido van Rossum, whose favorite comedy group was Monty Python's Flying Circus.

Qq

QA *n.* See Quality Assurance (QA).

QPL *n.* See Quality Products List (QPL).

qualified vendor *n.* A vendor determined by a buying organization to meet minimum set standards of business competence, reputation, financial ability and product quality for placement on the vendor list.

qualifier *n.* A data element that gives a generic data element a specific meaning. For example, EDI sender and receiver addresses are usually preceded by a Qualifier (i.e. 01:235621906; in this case 01 is the Qualifier).

quality *n.* The composite of material attributes, including performance features and characteristics, of a product or service to satisfy a given need.

Quality Assurance (QA) *n.* The design and implementation of systematic activities aimed at preventing quality problems. This is a common phase (generally towards the end) of an E-Procurement implementation to check and understand potential and existing problems.

---

quality control *n.* The activities and techniques used to achieve and maintain a high standard of quality in a transformation process. This may include systematic inspection of inputs and outputs, or a sample of inputs and outputs at various stages in their transformation to ensure that acceptable tolerances are not being exceeded.

quality of service *n.* Defines the level of service for an individual, voice, data or video connection when using a telecommunications carrier.

Quality Products List (QPL) *n.* A list of products that, because of the length of time required for test and evaluation, are tested in advance of procurement to determine which suppliers comply with the specification requirements. Also referred to as an "approved brands list."

quantity discount *n.* A price reduction to buyers who buy large volumes of a product.

query *v.* A question; to ask or seek. In information technology, what a user of a search engine or database enters is called a query. Languages used to interact with databases are called query languages; SQL (Structured Query Language) is a well-known standard.

Quetzal *n.* The standard monetary unit of Guatemala.

queue *n.* A line of processes or requests that are waiting to be handled by an application or operating system. This term is common in relation to an office's printer; printer jobs wait in the queue until each request is fulfilled respectively.

quick response *n.* A supply chain management philosophy in which business can respond quickly to customer orders. Analogous to Just-in-Time manufacturing.

Quicktime *n.* A multimedia development, storage, and playback technology from Apple. Quicktime files combine sound, text, animation, and video in a single file.

quid pro quo *n.* Latin for 'something for something'; something given as compensation for something received.

quiesce *v.* To put a computer, an application, a thread, or some other computer resource into a temporarily inactive or inhibited state. A resource that is in a quiesced state can be reactivated more quickly than one that has been completely removed from the system.

Rr

RAID *n.* An acronym for Redundant Array of Independent Disks; a way of storing the same data in different places and on multiple hard disks. A RAID appears to the operating system to be single logical hard disk. RAID employs the technique of striping, which involves partitioning each drive's storage space into units ranging from a sector (512 bytes) up to several megabytes. The stripes of all the disks are interleaved and addressed in order. By placing data on multiple disks, I/O operations can be balanced, improving performance.

RAM *n.* See random access memory (RAM).

Rand *n.* The standard monetary unit of South Africa and Namibia.

random access memory (RAM) *n.* The place in a computer where the operating system, application programs, and data in current use are kept so that they can be quickly reached by the computer's processes. RAM is much faster to read from and write to than other kinds of storage, but data is only stored as long as your computer is running.

rate of exchange *n.* The price of one currency in terms of another. It is usually expressed in terms of how many units of the home country's currency are needed to buy one unit of the foreign currency. Also known as an exchange rate.

---

ratification *v.* The process used by an agency's contracting officers to approve and legitimize an otherwise proper contract made by an individual without contracting authority.

rationalization *v.* A reorganization of a firm, group, or industry to increase its efficiency and profitability. This may include closing some manufacturing units and expanding others (horizontal integration), merging different stages of the production process (vertical integration), merging support units, closing units that are duplicating efforts of others, etc. An organization may also rationalize its product range to reflect changes in demand, concentrating its sales and marketing effort on its best sellers.

raw materials *n.* Direct materials used in a production process, which are at a low level of completion compared to the final product or cost unit. Examples include steel, wood, and chemicals.

RDBMS *n.* See relational database management system (RDBMS).

read-only memory (ROM) *n.* A type of computer main store memory whose contents may be read but not altered and are not lost when the computer is switched off.

Real *n.* The standard monetary unit of Brazil.

real-time processing *n.* The processing of data by a computer application as soon as it is input so that the results can be output almost immediately.

rebate *n.* A discount offered on the price of a good or service, often one that is paid back to the payer.

receipt *n.* A document acknowledging that a specified payment has been made.

receivables *n.* Sums of money due to a business from persons or businesses to whom it has supplied goods or services in the normal course of trade.

recourse agreement *n.* An agreement between a hire purchase company and a retailer, in which the retailer undertakes to repossess the goods if the buyer fails to pay his regular installments.

redundancy *n.* The loss of a job by an employee because his or her job has ceased to exist or because there is no longer work for him or her. It involves dismissal by the employer, with or without notice, for any reason other than a breach of the contract of employment by the employee, provided that the same employer has offered no reasonable alternative employment.

registration of interest *n.* A request issued by a customer for suppliers to nominate that they are interested in a particular project.

regular expression *n.* A way for a user to express how a computer program should look for a specified pattern of text. The author of a regular expression can then tell the program what it is to do when matching patterns are found. An example application that searches for regular expressions is grep, which is usually found on UNIX-based operating systems.

relational database management system (RDBMS) *n.* An application that allows you to create, updates, and administers a relational database. An RDBMS takes SQL statements entered by a user or contained in an application program and creates, updates, or provides access to the database. Examples of RDBMS systems include Oracle, and IBM's DB2.

relaunch *n.* To reintroduce an existing product or brand into the market after changes have been made to it.

remuneration *n.* A sum of money paid for a service given.

render *n.* The ability to form something out of something else originally given. In information technology, a monitor renders an image that is sent to it in the form of a bitmap or streaming image.

repudiation *n.* The refusal of one party to pay a debt or honor a contract; also breach of contract.

Request for Bid (RFB) *n.* A solicitation in which the terms, conditions, and specifications are described and responses are not subject to negotiation.

Request for Comments (RFC) *n.* A formal document from the Internet Engineering Task Force that is the result of committee drafting and subsequent review by interested parties. Some RFC's are informational, however many eventually become the final version of a standard and no further comments or changes are permitted.

Request for Information (RFI) *n.* A request issued by a customer for suppliers to provide additional information on a particular product or service.

Request for Offer (RFO) *n.* A request issued by a customer for offers to be provided by a supplier.

Request for Proposal (RFP) *n.* A request issued by a customer for proposals to be provided by a supplier.

requirements contract *n.* A form or contract that is used when the total long-term quantity required cannot be definitely fixed, but can be stated as an estimate or within maximum and minimum limits with deliveries on demand.

requisition *n.* An electronic list of items that a buyer has requested while following a specified procedure. This may include items from multiple suppliers. When a requisition is approved, a purchase order is generated to send to the supplier(s).

requisition template *n.* A type of requisition that can be used to create another requisition. A requisition template can contain items that are repeatedly ordered, or other types of information such as default billing, shipping, and approval information.

reserve price *n.* The lowest price a seller is willing to accept for an item offered for sale by public auction. If the reserve price is not reached by the bidding, the auctioneer is instructed to withdraw the item from sale.

resistance to change *n.* Antagonism towards change among the employees in an organization. Possible reasons for resistance includes a misunderstanding of the goal of the change, having a low tolerance of change (particularly through fear), and perceiving that something of value will be lost. Quick implementation of E-Procurement applications has made this scenario common in large organizations.

responder *n.* One who submits a response to a solicitation document.

return on investment (ROI) *n.* An accounting term expressing the profit of an organization for a financial year as a percentage of the capital employed. It is probably one of the most frequently used ratios for assessing the performance of the organization. There are many different ways to calculate this but the overall expected measurement is how much are we getting back for the money and resources we expended. Early implementations of E-Procurement systems expected immediate positive ROI, although that rarely happened.

returns to scale *n.* A concept where bigger is better. It's what creates the winner-take-all quality of most b-to-b hubs. It also places an advantage on being first to market and first to achieve critical mass.

revenue *n.* Any form of income; cost and income items that are either charged or credited to the profit and loss account for an accounting period.

reverse auction *n.* Suppliers, instead of buying companies, are in the bidding process for a purchasing contract, usually lowering the price significantly. Freemarkets.com is an exchange where buying organizations can participate in reverse auctions.

reverse engineering *n.* The process of taking apart an object to see how it works in order to duplicate or enhance the object. Someone doing reverse engineering on software may use several tools to disassemble a program. One tool is a hexadecimal dumper, which prints or displays the binary numbers of a program in hexadecimal format. These tools might be used by a cracker to modify code and gain entry to a computer system or cause other harm.

RFB *n.* See Request for Bid (RFB).

RFI *n.* See Request for Information (RFI).

RFO *n.* See Request for Offer (RFO).

RFP *n.* See Request for Proposal (RFP).

Rial *n.* The standard monetary unit of Iran and Oman.

Rich Text Format (RTF) *n.* A standard format (from Microsoft) for text that shows all of the formatting to be used on the text. Allows easy transfer of documents between different word processing applications.

right of resale *n.* The right that the seller in a contract of sale has to resell the goods if the buyer does not pay the price as agreed. If the goods are perishable or the seller tells the buyer that the goods will be resold and the buyer still does not pay within a reasonable time, the seller may resell them and recovers from the first buyer damages for any loss.

rightsizing *n.* The restructuring and rationalization of an organization to improve effectiveness and cut costs, without involving a full downsizing operation, that can often be overdone.

ring *n.* A number of manufacturers, dealers, or traders who agree among themselves to control the price or conditions of sale of a product for their own benefit.

Ringgit *n.* The standard monetary unit of Malaysia.

risk capital *n.* Capital invested in a project in which there is a substantial element of risk, especially money invested in new venture or an expanding business in exchange for shares in the business. Risk capital is normally invested in the equity of the company; it is not a loan. Also called venture capital.

Riyal *n.* The standard monetary unit of Saudi Arabia, Qatar, and Yemen.

rlogin *n.* Remote login is a UNIX command that allows an authorized user to login to other UNIX machines on a network and to interact as if the user were physically at the host computer. Once logged in to the host, the user can do anything that the host has given permission for, such as read, edit, or delete files.

Robinson-Patman Act (1936) *n.* A federal law intended to halt discriminatory pricing policies by specifying certain limited conditions under which a seller is permitted to charge different prices to different buyers.

ROI *n*. Abbreviation for Return on investment (ROI), also Registration of Interest (ROI).

rollback *n*. The undoing of partly completed database changes when a database transaction is determined to have failed.

rollout *n*. A staged series of activities that often accumulate meaning as they occur. Computer manufacturers use the term to describe a series of related product announcements that are staged over time. Often times during an e-procurement implementation, the final stage is to rollout the initial pilot system to the enterprise for organization-wide usage.

root directory *n*. In a computer file system that is organized as a hierarchy or tree, the root directory is the directory that includes all other directories. In UNIX operating systems, the root directory has no name, it's simply represented by the special character that separates directories in a file system. In UNIX-based systems, the root directory is represented as "/". In Windows systems, the root directory is represented as "\".

Rouble *n*. The standard monetary unit of Russia, Belarus, and Tajikistan.

round robin *n*. An arrangement of choosing all elements in a group equally in some rational order. A way to think about round robin is that it's about "taking turns." An enterprise application that uses multiple web servers (to distribute the load), the developers may use a type of "round robin DNS" which allows requests to be served by every web server.

router *n*. A special -purpose computer (or software package) that handles the connection between 2 or more networks. Routers spend all their time looking at the destination addresses of the packets passing

---

through them and deciding which route to send them on.

runtime *n.* Refers to the time when a program or application is running. When you start a program running on a computer, it is runtime for that program.

Rupee *n.* The standard monetary unit of India, Pakistan, Nepal, Sri Lanka, Mauritius, and Seychelles.

Ss

S/MIME *n.* See Single Multi-Purpose Internet Mail Extensions (S/MIME).

safe mode *n.* A way to book up Window's operating systems in a way that makes it easier to diagnose problems. No startup programs are loaded other than the operating system and driver for the mouse, keyboard, and display modes display.

Samba *n.* A popular freeware program that allows end users to access and use files, printers, and other shared resources on a company's intranet. Samba is popular because it's not operating system dependent; resources across the network can be shared regardless of the operating system it's running on.

sandbox 1. *n.* An area or infrastructure in a company's enterprise that is used for development and/or testing new technologies. This is regarded as an area where if failures occur, it won't damage other applications that are mission-critical. Developers often play in the sandbox. 2. *n.* Using the Java programming language and development environment, the sandbox is the program area and set of rules that programmers need to use when creating java code.

SAP *n.* A corporation based in Germany, which provides software to

---

manage financial, asset, and cost accounting, production operations and materials, personnel, plants, and archived documents. SAP has over 20,000 employees based in over 50 countries.

SAS *n.* See single award schedule (SAS).

salary *n.* A regular payment, usually bi-weekly, made by an employer, under a contract of employment, to an employee.

sale and leaseback *n.* A transaction in which the owner of an asset sells it and immediately purchases it back from the buyer the right to use the asset under a lease.

sale as seen *n.* A sale made on the basis that the buyer has inspected the goods and is buying them as a result of this inspection and not on any guarantee of quality or condition by the seller. The seller does not guarantee or imply that the goods are suitable for any particular purpose.

sale by description *n.* A sale made on the basis that the quality of the goods sold will correspond to the description given of them in the contract of sale.

sale by sample *n.* A sale made on the basis of sample, in other words that the quality and condition of the bulk of the goods will be at least as good as that of the selling sample. In contracts in which goods are sold by sample, the contract may stipulate how and by whom the bulk should be sampled and what tests should be used to compare it to the selling sample. The contract will also usually lay down the procedure to be adopted if the bulk sample is not as good as the selling sample.

sale or return *n.* Terms of trade in which the seller agrees to take back from the buyer any unsold goods, usually in a specified period.

sales invoice *n.* A document sent by the seller of goods or services to the buyer, detailing the amounts due, discounts available, payment dates, and such details as the account numbers and credit limits.

sample *n.* A small quantity of a commodity, etc., selected to represent the bulk of a quantity of goods.

SAX *n.* See Simple API for XML (SAX).

scalability *n.* The ability of a computer application or program to continue to function properly when changed in size or volume in order to meet an enterprises' needs. The biggest unanswered question after a pilot implementation of an e-procurement system is will the system be scalable for the entire enterprise? In other words, will it handle an excessive amount of user requests and still perform up to scale.

scalable *adj.* The ability of a system to be easily expanded to meet future demands.

Scan-Based Trading (SBT) *n.* Scan-based trading is a fundamental change in the way manufacturers and retailers conduct business. It rewards both trading partners through synchronized information systems, shared revenue point and shrink cost and elimination of non-value costs.

scenario *n.* A means of attempting to forecast developments in an industry by using expert opinion to formulate a qualitative view of the future. It should identify major trends and analyze long term environmental influences. Many factors need to be balanced against each other to produce a range of possible scenarios. From the final scenario managers should be able to examine the strategic options and challenge existing assumptions and practices.

schedule *n.* A plan of activities that uses the resources made available by aggregate planning and allocates them to individual jobs, activities, or customers over a particular period. A schedule shows what has to be done, when, by whom, and with what resources. If the output of the system is being made to order, the schedule provides detailed timings for each order. If the output is being made to stock inventory, it provides detailed timings for products.

schema *n.* The organization or structure for a database. The term sometimes seems to refer to a visualization of a structure and sometimes to a formal text-oriented description. When someone requests a database schema, they want a visual representation of how the tables and relationships are laid out.

Schilling *n.* The standard monetary unit of Austria.

SCOR *n.* Supply Chain Operations Reference model; a methodology for supply chain improvement developed by the Supply-Chain Council. PLAN -> SOURCE -> MAKE -> DELIVER -> RETURN.

search-engine *n.* A service provided on the internet that enables the user to search for items of interest. Some such services are free and attempt to capture information from the whole range of material available on the net (e.g. Yahoo, Google). Others are subscription-based but in return provide access to specialist publications, full-text retrieval capabilities, or other added-value services.

search-and-replace *n.* A capability that allows a computer user to find a given sequence of characters in one or more text files. A global search-and-replace means that the replace operation is to take effect in all files within the context of the search.

seasonal rate *n.* A rate of charging that varies according to the time of the year.

second-level domain *n.* A portion of a web browser's URL (Uniform Resource Locator) that identifies the specific and unique administrative owner associated with an IP address. For example, for the web address www.rockbend.com, 'rockbend' is the second-level domain.

Secure Multi-Purpose Internet Mail Extensions (S/MIME) *n.* A secure method of sending email messages that uses the Rivest-Shamir-Adleman encryption system. RSA has proposed S/MIME as a standard to the Internet Engineering Task Force.

secure shell (ssh) *n.* A UNIX-based command interface and protocol for securely getting access to a remote computer. It's widely used by system administrators to control servers remotely with a certain guarantee of privacy.

Secure Sockets Layer (SSL) *n.* A protocol that uses encryption to transmit secure documents on the internet. Web pages using an SSL connection begin with the identifier "https" instead of "http".

segment *n.* A predefined set of functionally related data elements that make up a specific unit in an EDI transaction set. A segment is essentially one line of data within an EDI document.

segment terminator *n.* The control character that marks the end of a specific variable-length segment. This character would be different from the delimiter, yet would not appear in the body of the message. A common segment terminator is the tilde.

self-actualization *n.* The drive people have to realize their potential and to be fulfilled in their work. It encompasses the human need for challenge, responsibility, and variety at work, enabling employees to take pride in their achievements, as well as in their technical or professional expertise. An integral part of the concept is for their worth to be recognized and valued by those with, and for, whom they work.

sell-side procurement model *n.* A web site produced and managed by a vendor company that allows buyers to browse and purchase their products. All catalog and pricing data is managed by the vendor.

The obvious disadvantage to this system is the ability of the buyer to update their internal ERP and reporting systems with relevant purchasing details. Many times, the individual buyer has to re-key this information manually into the target system.

seller's market *n.* A market in which the demand exceeds the supply, so that sellers can increase prices. At some point, however, buyers will cease to follow the price raises and the sellers will be forced to drop prices in order to make sales.

semantics *n.* A term used in computer programming, it refers to what the words really say or what functions are requested in the command.

semaphore *n.* A technique for coordinating or synchronizing activities in which multiple processes compete for the same operating system resources. A semaphore is a value in a designated place in operating system storage that each process can check and then change. Semaphore settings on the Solaris operating system are in a file called "/etc/system".

sendmail *n.* The most popular UNIX-based implementation of the Simple Mail Transfer Protocol (SMTP) for transmitting e-mail. Sendmail is available on most UNIX operating systems.

separator character *n.* A character used for the syntactical separation of data. Also known as a delimiter. Common separators are commas or tab marks.

server *n.* A computer, or a software package, that provides a specific kind of service to client software running on other computers. The term can refer to a particular piece of software, such as a World Wide Web server, or to the machine on which the software is running.

server farm *n.* A group of computers acting as servers and housed together in a single location. A server farm is sometimes called a server cluster. In a business environment, a server farm or cluster might perform such services as providing centralized access control, file access, printer sharing, and backup for workstation users. On the internet, a web server farm may refer to a web site that uses two or more servers to handle user requests.

server-side include *n.* A variable value that a server can include in an HTML file before it sends it to the requestor. A common example of a server-side include is the "last modified date" time stamp. Last modified is one of the environment variables that an operating system can keep track of and that can be accessible to a server program. The server-side include in the HTML file finds the value of that variable, and puts it into the file that is eventually delivered to the user.

servlet *n.* A small program written in Java that runs on a server. The advantage of a Java servlet on servers with lots of traffic is that they can execute more quickly than comparable CGI applications. Rather than causing a separate program process to be created, each user request is invoked as a thread in a single daemon process, meaning that the amount of system overhead for each request is minimal.

session *n.* A series of interactions between two communications end points that occur during the span of a single connection. A connection is maintained while the two end points are communicating back and forth in a conversation or session of some duration. Examples include a telnet session (user logging into a server) or a user session in a web application (duration of time for the user to interact with information resources provided by the application).

set-aside *n.* Procurement systems, or parts, which are for the exclusive participation of small business, minority business, and/or labor surplus area firms.

settlement agreement *n.* A written agreement, in the form of a modification to a contract, settling all or a severable portion of a settlement proposal resulting from termination of a contract for the convenience of the agency.

SGML *n.* See Standard Generalized Markup Language (SGML).

shared hosting *n.* Web hosting in which the service provider serves pages for multiple web sites, each having its own internet domain name, from a single web server. Most web hosting companies provide shared hosting. This type of web hosting model may not appropriate for high-traffic sites.

shareware *n.* Computer software, distributed through public domain channels, for which the author expects to receive minimal compensation. Examples include games, ftp clients, and word-processing programs.

shell *n.* An interactive user interface found on UNIX-based operating systems. The shell is the layer of programming that understands and executes the commands a user enters. Common shells include Korn, Bourne, and C shell.

shell script *n.* A text file that contains a sequence of commands for a UNIX-based operating system. A shell script is usually created for command sequences for which a user has a repeated need. It's initiated by entering the name of the shell script on a command line.

Sheqel *n.* The standard monetary unit of Israel.

shipping method *n.* A specification on how merchandise is shipped from a supplier organization to a buyer organization; e.g. Federal Express or UPS Next Day.

shopping cart *n.* On a web site that sells products online, the shopping cart is a metaphor for the catalog or other pages where a user reads and makes selections. After selection is complete, the user goes to an order confirmation screen to "checkout" all of the items collected in the shopping cart.

short delivery *n.* A delivery of goods that has fewer items than invoiced or a smaller total weight than invoiced. This may be due to accidental loss, which could give rise to an insurance claim, or it may be due to some normal process, such as drying out during shipment, in which case the weight on arrival will be used in a final invoice. It may also be an attempt by the seller to make an extra profit, in which case the buyer would be well advised to make a claim for short delivery.

show stopper *n.* An unexpected result or the inability to meet a customer's core requirement when providing a product or service. For example, there can be a number of showstoppers when implementing an E-Procurement system because the new functionality may not mirror previous standard processes.

SIC *n.* See Standard Industrial Classification (SIC).

signature file *n.* A short text file for use as a standard attachment or appendage at the end of your e-mail messages.

silicon alley *n.* A community of Internet and computer-oriented businesses in the New York metropolitan area, particularly in Manhattan.

Simple API for XML (SAX) *n.* An application program interface that allows a programmer to interpret a web file that uses the Extensible Markup Language (XML). SAX is an event-driven interface. The developer specifies an event that may happen and, if it does, SAX handles the situation.

Simple Mail Transfer Protocol (SMTP) *n.* The protocol used for transmitting electronic mail on the Internet.

single award schedule (SAS) *n.* SAS cover contracts made with one supplier at a stated price for delivery to geographic areas as defined in the schedule. Unit prices are established on a zonal basis to provide for differences in transportation.

single-product strategy *n.* A strategy that involves a company offering only one product or one product version with very few options. Few organizations find themselves using this strategy because the risks are too high (if the single product fails).

single source *n.* An acquisition where, after a search, only one supplier is determined to be reasonably available for the required product, service or construction item.

SKU *n.* See Stock Keeping Unit.

SMBXML *n.* An acronym for Small Business Extensible Markup Language; an open XML-based standard, designed specifically for use by small and medium-sized businesses, that describes a data exchange format for use in common business applications. The SMBXML specification includes elements intended primarily for transactions and recordkeeping.

SMTP *n.* See Simple Mail Transfer Protocol (SMTP).

sniffer *n.* A program that monitors and analyzes network traffic, detecting bottlenecks and problems. It can also be used to capture data being transmitted on a network.

soft currency *n.* The currency of a country that has a weak balance of payments and for which there is relatively little demand.

software package *n.* A set of computer programs that work together to achieve a specific purpose; for example an accounting package or office software package.

Solaris *n.* A UNIX-based operating system developed by Sun Microsystems.

sole source procurement *n.* A contract for the purchase of supplies or services that is entered into by an agency after soliciting and negotiating with only one source. Such procurements must be fully justified to indicate the reasons why competition is not possible.

solicitation *n.* The process used to communicate procurement requirements and to request responses from interested vendors. A solicitation may be, but is not limited to a request for bid and request for proposal.

source code *n.* Programming statements that are created by a programmer with a text editor or visual programming tool and then saved in a file. When you purchase application software, it is usually in the form of compiled code and the source code is not included.

source document *n.* The first document to record a transaction.

source reduction product *n.* A product that results in a net reduction in the generation of waste, and includes durable, reusable and remanufactured products; products with no packaging or reduced packaging.

source selection plan *n.* The document that explains how proposals from offerors will be evaluated. The Plan includes the evaluation factors to be used, relative weight of the factors, and the methodology to be used by evaluators in evaluating proposals.

sourcing *n.* Refers to the selection of vendors an organization chooses to do business with. See Strategic Sourcing.

SPARC *n.* An acronym for Scalable Processor Architecture; a 32 and 64 bit microprocessor architecture from Sun Microsystems that is based on reduced instruction set computing (RISC). SPARC is a widely used architecture for hardware used with UNIX-based operating systems, including Sun's Solaris.

specification *n.* A concise statement of a set of requirements to be satisfied by a product, material or process that indicates whenever appropriate the procedures to determine whether the requirements are satisfied. As far as practicable, it is desirable that the requirements are expressed numerically in terms of appropriate units, together with their limits. A specification may be a standard, a part of a standard, or independent of a standard.

splash page *n.* An initial web page used to capture the user's attention for a short time as a promotion or lead-in to the site home page or to tell the user what kind of browser and other software plug-in's required to view the site.

spoof *n.* The process of faking an Internet address so that one looks like a certain kind of internet user. It's particularly easy to spoof an e-mail address using e-mail applications such as UNIX-based Sendmail.

spoofing *v.* See Spoof.

sporadic problem *n.* A short-term non-random problem that may cause a process to deviate from its control limits. Many new releases of E-Business applications may have sporadic problems due to its immaturity.

spreadsheet *n.* A computer application used for numerical tabular operations, such as financial forecasting and planning. It displays a large table of columns and rows. Numbers are entered by the user to show, for example, financial results or items of income an expenditure.

If instructed, the spreadsheet can automatically calculate those numbers that are derived from figures already entered. The application can also update the figures shown in all columns when the user changes a single figure.

SQL *n.* See Structured Query Language (SQL).

stand-alone computer *n.* A self-contained computer that can be operated without having to be connected to a central computing facility or to a network. Stand-alone computers are useful for information that has been recognized as security-intensive.

standard deviation 1. *n.* The amount of forecast error or variance from the mathematical mean. 2. *n.* How close the forecast is to the actual demand for products or goods, expressed as a percentage.

Standard Generalized Markup Language (SGML) *n.* A language that uses tags embedded in text to mark up the text. This allows the text to be read by specific client software that can translate the tags into formats, links, graphics, etc. XML is considered a slim-down version of SGML.

Standard Industrial Classification (SIC) *n.* Classification of business established by type of activity for the purpose of facilitating the collection, tabulation, presentation, and analysis of data collected by various agencies of the United States government, state agencies, trade associations, and private research organizations for promoting uniformity and comparability in the presentation of statistical data relating to those establishments and their fields of endeavor.

standard purchase price *n.* A predetermined price set for each commodity of direct material for a specified period.

standardization *n.* The process of defining and applying the conditions necessary to ensure that a given range of requirements can normally be met, with a minimum of variety, in a reproducible and economic manner based on the best current techniques.

static *n.* Stationary or fixed; e.g. a static web page is pre-formatted and has no capacity to return information.

static IP address *n.* An IP address usually allocated to a computer system that will never move. Computer workstations and servers usually have constant IP addresses that are rarely changed.

stickiness *adj.* A slang term to describe the attributes of a web site to attract and keep users in the area. Also a measurement of how many users return to the site for more information or products.

stock keeping unit (SKU) *n.* A unique alphanumeric code that subdivides a product into more specific categories; e.g. different colors of an envelope will each have a unique SKU identifier. A SKU is not the same as a manufacturer part number or product code, although the model number could for all or part of the SKU. The merchant establishes the SKU, whereas the manufacturer decides a part number.

stockpile *n.* An unusually large stock of a raw material held by an organization in anticipation of a shortage, transport strike, planned production increase, etc.

straight rebuy *v.* Business buyer behavior characterized by automatic and regular repurchasing of familiar products from regular suppliers.

Structured Query Language (SQL) *n.* A standard interactive and programming language for getting information from and updating a database. Queries take the form of a command language that lets you select, insert, update, find out the location of data, and so forth.

SQL> select * from USER_NAME;

This example shows an SQL statement that reads all of the entries in the USER_NAME table and prints them back to the screen.

StarOffice *n.* A free office-application suite from Sun Microsystems that includes a word processor, spreadsheet, database, presentation maker, illustrator, schedule management, and e-mail component. StarOffice is compatible with Microsoft Office components and similar in functionality.

stateless *adj.* An adjective that describes whether a computer application is designed to note and remember one or more preceding events in a given sequence of interactions with a user, another computer or program, a device, or other outside element. It means there is no record of previous interactions and each interaction request has to be handled based entirely on the information that comes with it.

strategic sourcing *n.* The process of understanding exactly what, and from whom the company is buying, and at what price, then, deciding which vendors should be allowed to participate in the selling process to your organization. Many times a negotiated discount between the buyer and seller decides the sourcing process. However, auctions and market exchanges make the process of strategic sourcing less important.

string *n.* A sequence of symbols or values, such as a character string (a sequence of characters) or a binary digit string.

stylesheet *n.* A definition of a document's appearance in terms of typeface, document layout, line spacing, and margin width's. For web pages, a stylesheet allows the designer to ensure an underlying consistency across a site's pages.

subcontract *n.* A contract between a prime contractor and another source to obtain outside supplies for services that prime contractor reeds to perform the contract requirements. Subcontracts include any agreement, other than an employer employee relationship, which a prime contractor enters into for the purpose of fulfilling a government contract.

subnet *n.* An identifiably separate part of an organization's network. Having an organization's network divided into subnets allows it to be connected to the Internet with a single shared network address. Without subnets, an organization would have multiple connections to the Internet, one for each separate network, but would require an unnecessary use of the limited number of network numbers the Internet has to assign.

supplier *n.* An organization that owns and sells products through a catalog.

supply chain *n.* A series of linked stages in a supply network along which a particular set of goods or services flows. See Supply Chain Management.

Supply Chain Execution (SCE) *n.* The ability to move the product out the warehouse door. This is a critical capacity and one that only brick-and-mortar firms bring to the B2B table. Dot-coms have the technology, but that's only part of the equation. The need for SCE is what is driving the dotcom's to offer equity partnerships to the wholesale distributors.

Supply Chain Integration (SCI) *n.* Likely to become a key competitive advantage of selected e-marketplaces. Similar concept to the Back-End Integration, but with greater emphasis on the moving of goods and services.

Supply Chain Management (SCM) *n.* The management of the links between an organization and its suppliers. There are specialist companies that offer to manage the whole of the supply chain, on behalf of manufacturers. Supply chain management covers: *Materials management* The management of the flow of materials through an organizations supply chain, including suppliers, inventory management, operations planning and control, and distribution to customers. *Logistics* The management of materials and information flows from the organization to its customers. *Physical distribution management* The management of the process that connects the producer and the first-tier customers, including storage and transport. *Purchasing and supply management* The management of an organization's interface with suppliers, ensuring that the right quantity is bought at the right time, at the right price, to the right quality specification, and from the right sources. *Information flow management* The management of the flow of information between an organization and both its suppliers and its customers. For every unit of material flow in one direction through the supply chain, there should be at least one corresponding information flow in the opposite direction. Some recent improvements in materials management have come from the use of computers and information technology in the flow of information.

swap file *n.* A space on a hard disk used as the virtual memory extension of a computer's real memory (RAM). Having a swap file allows your computer's operating system to pretend that you have more RAM than you actually do.

switching cost *n.* A means of building a competitive advantage into a product or service by involving buyers in an extra cost if they switch to an alternative supplier. It may form part of the physical characteristics of the product, which make it incompatible with the equipment of alternative suppliers, or the switching cost may result from the disruption of the quality of service formed by a long-established and close working relationship.

synchronization *n.* The concept that all supply chain functions are integrated and interact in real time. When changes are made to one area, the effect is automatically reflected throughout the supply chain.

synchronous *n.* Occurring with a regular or predictable time relationship. Purchase order approval is generally in a synchronous cycle; e.g. if an order requires approval from the employee's manager and the CEO, the order must first be approved by the manager. If approved, it is forwarded to the CEO.

synergy *n*. The effects of different parts working together. A common term used when a company re-organization is announced.

syntax *n*. The grammar, structure, or order of the elements in a language statement. A computer language's syntax is considered its "word order", or rules, which govern how elements of the language relate to each other.

Tt

T1 *n.* A common digital line in the United States and Canada to access the internet. T1 lines use copper wire and span distances within and between major metropolitan areas.

tag *n.* A generic term for a language element descriptor, HTML is a tagged language. The set of tags for a document or other unit of information is sometimes referred to as markup.

Tagged Image File Format (TIFF) *n.* A format for graphics files.

Taguchi methods *n.* Methods of testing the design of a new product or service in the most extreme circumstances likely to occur. In theory, all possible design variables and combinations are investigated to achieve the optimum combination.

Taka *n.* The standard monetary unit of Bangladesh.

tar *n.* An acronym for tape archive; a UNIX shell command that creates a single file called an archive. A tar archive has the file suffix ".tar". The files in a tar archive are not compressed, just sewn together in one file.

---

target costing *v.* A methodology of costing new products. Subtracting the desired profit from the market price produces the target cost (Target cost = market price - desired profit).

task 1. *n.* An existing computer process, also known as a running application. 2. *n.* The smallest unit of work that can be assigned to an individual workstation.

Taxware *n.* A software application to calculate taxes.

tcl/tk *n.* An interpreted script language from Sun Microsystems. TK (toolkit) is a companion program which helps to create a graphical user interface with Tcl.

TCP/IP *n.* See Transfer Control Protocol/Internet Protocol (TCP/IP).

technological change *n.* An increase in the level of output resulting from automation and computerized methods of production. Apart from increasing output, technological change can affect the ratio of capital to labor used in a factory or information center. Many times it will result in a reduction of labor force.

telnet *n.* A portion of the TCP/IP suite of software protocols that handles terminals. Among other functions, it allows a user to log in to a remote computer from the user's local computer.

% telnet mail.rockbend.com

The result of this request would be an invitation to log on with a username and password into Rockbend.com's mail server.

temporal method *n.* A method of converting a foreign currency involved in a transaction in which the local currency is translated at the exchange rate in operation on the date which the transaction occurred. If rates do not fluctuate significantly, an average for the period may be used as an approximation.

tender *n.* A means of auctioning an item of value to the highest bidder.

term *n.* A clause in a contract that refers to a particular obligation between the contracting parties.

terminal *n.* Any personal computer or user workstation that is hooked up to a network. It usually refers to a workstation computer whose sole purpose is to access a large computer (e.g. mainframe or server).

terms and conditions *n.* A phrase generally applied to the rules under which all bids must be submitted and the stipulations included in most purchase contracts; often published by the purchasing authorities for the information of all potential vendors.

third-line forcing *v.* Forcing a buyer to take a supply of products he does not want as a condition of supplying him with a product he wants.

thrashing *n.* A computer activity that makes little or no progress, usually because memory or other resources have become exhausted or too limited to perform needed operations.

throughput *n.* A term usually related to a computer or application's ability to perform quickly. A benchmark can be used to measure throughput. If a web application is performing very slowly, you might overhear someone saying "I've got no throughput."

TIFF *n.* See Tagged Image File Format (TIFF).

tilde *n.* A character that looks like this: ~. The tilde is a common delimiter, or character separator in EDI transmissions.

time rate *n.* A rate of pay expressed as a sum of money paid to an individual for the time worked, rather than for a specified output;

compares to piece rate.

top-level domain *n.* A domain that identifies the most general part of the domain-name in an internet address. For example, "com" for commercial, "edu" for education, and "fr" for France are top-level domains.

tort *n.* A wrongful act, other than a breach of contract, such that the law permits compensation of damages.

total standard cost *n.* The total standard production cost plus the standard cost allowance for the non-production overhead.

traceroute *n.* A utility that record the route through the internet between your computer and a specified destination computer. It also calculates and displays the amount of time each hop took.

TRADACOMS *n.* Trading Data Communications Standards; British standards defined for EDI exchange that was primarily used in the automotive industry.

trade discount *n.* A reduction on the recommended prices of a product or service that is offered to distributors because they buy regularly in bulk. The difference between the retail price and the discounted price provides the buyer with his overheads and profit.

trading partner *n.* In a broad sense, any organizations doing business. The more specific EDI terminology are companies who agree to send and receive between each other with specific EDI messages.

trading partner agreement *n.* The written contract that spells out agreed upon terms between EDI trading partners.

transaction *n.* In computer programming, a transaction means a sequence of information exchange and related work that is treated as a unit for the purposes of satisfying a request and for ensuring database integrity. An order isn't a transaction until all the required steps are finished.

transaction set *n.* An EDI standard syntax consisting of a set of data segments that, taken together, comprise a single commercial transaction.

transaction set detail area *n.* The set of EDI standard segments, which contain information relating to the line items in the transaction set.

transfer pricing *n.* Setting a price for the internal transfer of raw materials, components, finished product, or services between the profit centers or trading units of an organization. The price charged may reflect the market price or be based on cost plus an agreed mark-up.

transmission *n.* The sending of data from one computer system to another.

transmission acknowledgement *n.* The acknowledgment that the total transmission was received with no errors detected (e.g. Message Disposition Notification (MDN)).

Transfer Control Protocol/Internet Protocol (TCP/IP) *n.* TCP/IP is a combined set of protocols that performs the transfer of data between two computers. TCP monitors and ensures correct transfer of data. IP receives the data from TCP, breaks it up into packets, and ships it off to a network within the Internet. TCP/IP is also used as a name for a protocol suite that incorporates these functions and others.

translation *n.* The use of maps to convert data from one format to another. For example, proprietary file formats are often translated into standard EDI record formats.

translator *n.* An application that performs the translation from one application format to another. Common translators include Mercator, and Gentran.

trigger *n.* In a database, a trigger is a set of SQL statement that automatically executes an action when a specific operation, such as an update of a table, occurs.

Trojan Horse *n.* A program in which harmful code is contained inside apparently harmless programming or data in such a way that it can get control and do damage. The term comes from the large wooden horse found in Homer's *Iliad*.

truncate *n.* To shorten and cut off. In information technology, when information is truncated, it is ended abruptly at a certain spot.

Tugrik *n.* The standard monetary unit of Mongolia.

turnkey system *n.* A computer system or application that is ready to start work as soon as it is installed. All the necessary programs and equipment are supplied with the system. This is a common marketing term for many E-Business applications, yet many times its not completely accurate description of their product or service.

typeface *n.* A design for a set of printer or display fonts, each for a set of characters, in a number of specific sizes.

Uu

UCC *n.* Uniform Code Council; a U.S. organization that defines rules, such as what constitutes a contract, what is evidence, and what is a signature for business transactions. The organization administers the Uniform Code Standard, the Universal Product Code and other EDI standards. The UCC assigns the first six digits of the UPC number; the vendor assigns the remaining five.

ullage *n.* The amount by which the full capacity of a barrel or similar container exceeds the volume of the contents, as a result of evaporation or leakage.

UML *n.* See Unified Modeling Language (UML).

UN/EDIFACT *n.* See United Nations EDI for Administration, Commerce, and Transport (UN/EDIFACT).

UN/SPSC and UNSPSC *n.* The Universal Standard Products and Services Classification (UNSPSC) is an open global coding system that classifies products and services. The UNSPSC is used extensively around the world in the electronic catalogs, search engines, procurement application systems and accounting systems. There is a significant difference between UN/SPSC and UNSPSC explained below (taken directly from unspsc.org):

The United Nations Standard Products and Services Codes (UN/SPSC) is a classification system based on the United Nations Common Coding System (UNCCS), designed by UNDP/IAPSO and the Standard Product and Services Code (SPSC) designed by Dun and Bradstreet. The UNDP claims ownership to the copyright of the UN/SPSC and it cannot be used or distributed without a license.

The Universal Standard Products and Services Classification (UNSPSC) is a global standard developed and managed through ECCMA by volunteer domain experts from around the world. The UNSPSC is in the public domain and it can be used and distributed without restrictions or license fees.

unamortized cost *n.* The value given to a fixed asset in the accounts of an organization after a reevaluation subtracting the total depreciation shown against that asset since it was revalued.

unauthorized commitment *n.* The placing of an order, orally or in writing, for supplies or service by an agency employee who does not have a contracting officer warrant authorizing them to enter into a contract on the behalf of the agency. Unauthorized commitments also include orders placed by contracting officers that exceed their authorized dollar limit.

uncompressing *n.* The process of expanding a compression file into its original form, usually files with the extension ".zip" or ".tar.Z".

uncontrollable costs *n.* Items of expenditure appearing on a manager's management accounting statement that are not able to be controlled or influenced by that level of management.

unicode *n.* A character language which provides a unique number for every character, no matter what the platform, no matter what the program, no matter what the language. All browsers and e-procurement applications should have Unicode support in order to support different languages and display of currencies.

Unified Modeling Language (UML) *n.* A standard notation for the modeling of objects as a first step in developing an object-oriented design methodology.

Uninterruptible Power Supply (UPS) *n.* A device that allows your computer to keep running for at least a short time when the primary power source is lost.

unit conversion table *n.* The ability to convert and interchange units of measure; e.g. 1 case equals 24 cans.

unit price *n.* The price of a selected unit of a good or service (e.g., pound, labor hours, etc.); the price paid per unit of item purchased or charged per unit of product sold.

United Nations EDI for Administration, Commerce, and Transport (UN/EDIFACT) *n.* An EDI message standard. See also EDIFACT.

UNIX *n.* An operating system that originated at Bell Labs in 1969 as an interactive time-sharing system. UNIX is a popular operating system on the Internet due to its maturity, and low level of system resources required to run it.

unsettled contract change *n.* Any pending contract change or contract term for which a modification is required, to include a change order that has not been negotiated, but has been affected.

unsolicited proposal *n.* A written proposal that is submitted to an agency by an outside source offering to perform an agency's work more effectively or efficiently. The unsolicited proposal shall not be in response to a formal or informal request, unless it is an agency request constituting a publicized general statement of need.

URL *n.* An acronym for Uniform Resource Locator; the address of a file (resource) accessible on the Internet. The URL contains the name of the protocol (e.g. http, ldap) required to access the resource, a domain name that identifies a specific computer on the Internet, and a description of a file location on the computer.

UPS *n.* See uninterruptible power supply (UPS).

usability *n.* The measure of a product's potential to accomplish the goals of the user. Usability testing is a method by which users of product are asked to perform certain tasks in an effort to measure the products ease-of-use, task duration, and the user's perception of the experience. Often, e-procurement usability tests ask the users to accomplish all of the tasks, which they're required to do now on their client/server based model.

usury *n.* An excessively high rate of interest.

Vv

validation *n.* The process of determining that compliance standards have been met by a particular document in a transmission. XML documents are commonly validated against a document type definition.

valorization *n.* The raising or stabilization of the value of a commodity or currency by artificial means, usually by a government. For example, if a government wishes to increase the price of a commodity that it exports it may attempt to decrease the supply of that commodity by encouraging producers to produce less.

Value Added Network (VAN) *n.* A telecommunications network providing communication facilities that enhance basic telecommunications services.

value analysis *n.* An organized effort directed at analyzing the function of systems, products, specifications, standards, practices, and procedures for the purpose of satisfying the required function at the lowest total cost of effective ownership consistent with the requirements for performance, reliability, quality and maintenance.

value chain *n.* The chain of activities by which a company buys in materials, creates a good or service, markets it, and provides services after a sale is made. Each step creates more value for the consumer.

value chain analysis *n.* The use of structured design methods to define information related to the activities performed by all partners across an entire industry supply chain.

value engineering *n.* An organized effort to analyze the functions of systems, equipment, facilities, services, and supplies for the purpose of achieving the essential functions at the lowest life cycle cost consistent with required performance, reliability, quality, and safety.

variable 1. *adj.* A characteristic of a product or service that can be measured on a continuously variable scale, e.g. length, weight, etc. 2. *n.* A computing term meaning a value that isn't consistent, may change in the future.

variable cost *n.* An item of expense that, in total, varies directly with the level of activity achieved. For example, direct materials cost will tend to double if output doubles.

VAN *n.* See Value Added Network (VAN).

variable length field *n.* A data element that have characters which may range over a specified minimum and maximum length. Only meaningful characters in the field are transmitted. All public EDI standards are of variable length.

VBScript *n.* An interpreted script language developed by Microsoft which is a subset of the Visual Basic programming language. In general, script languages are easier to use and faster to code than compiled languages.

vendor *n.* A person or organization who sells goods or services. See supplier.

vendor code *n.* A unique identifier, usually a number and sometimes the company's DUNS number, assigned by a customer from the vendor it buys from.

vendors list *n.* A list of names and addresses of suppliers from whom bids, proposals and quotations might be expected. The list, maintained by the purchasing office, should include all suppliers who have expressed interest in doing business with the government.

Vendor Managed Inventory (VMI) *n.* A different approach to the traditional replenishment cycle, VMI uses EDI transactions, but unlike EDI, which merely automates existing work tasks, it eliminates work and tasks. It completely eliminates routine, repetitive purchasing activities for both the distributor and the manufacturer providing the program. The distributor retains control of his inventory by setting the objectives for service level or inventory investment. The manufacturer's computer operates the process, and measures the joint progress toward the objectives. The intended result is the achieving of the distributor's targeted service level to the end customer at the lowest possible total cost over time.

vertical market *n.* A particular industry or group of enterprises in which similar products or services are developed and marketed using similar methods. Vertical marketplaces are popular within the automotive and manufacturing industries.

VMI *n.* See Vendor Managed Inventory.

Voice Markup Language (VoxML) *n.* A technology developed by Motorola for creating a voice dialog with a web site in which a user can call a web site by phone and interact with it through speech recognition and web site responses.

vortal *n.* A vertical industry portal that provides a gateway to information related to a particular industry, such as automobiles or food manufacturing.

W3C *n.* An industry consortium which seeks to promote standards for the web and interoperability between products by producing specifications and reference software. All material at the W3C is freely available at http://www.w3c.org.

WAN *n.* See Wide Area Network (WAN).

WAP *n.* An acronym for Wireless Application Protocol; a specification for a set of communication protocols to standardize the way wireless devices, such as cellular telephones, can be used for Internet access.

warehouse *n.* Any building in which goods are stored; a public warehouse is one at or near a port in which goods are stored after being unloaded from a ship or before being loaded onto a ship.

web marketplaces *n.* An electronic marketplace in which goods, services, and financial instruments are traded. Exchanges have been revitalized on the Internet by connecting individual and large communities of buyers and sellers. Web marketplaces can be global and operate on a 24/7 basis. Such exchanges have the intrinsic advantage of exposing true cost, value, and price and tend to eliminate the waste and inefficiencies. The resulting savings can be shared among buyers, sellers, and exchanges.

---

webmaster *n.* An individual in an organization that manages the information content, and oversees the server and technical programming of a web site. Depending on the size of your organization, it can mean different responsibilities. In larger organizations, webmaster tend to have specific responsibilities regarding specific sites. In small organizations, this individual may have to "do it all," all web-related activities would fall under this person's responsibilities.

white goods *n.* A group of consumer durables that includes washing machines, dishwashers, refrigerators, dryers, freezers, and stoves; they are named white goods because they are usually finished in white enamel paint.

white paper *n.* 1. An article that states an organization's position or philosophy about a social, political, or other subject. 2. A high-level technical explanation of an architecture, framework, or product technology.

wholesaler *n.* A distributor that sells goods in large quantities, usually to other distributors. Typically, a wholesaler buys and stores large quantities of several producers' goods and breaks into the bulk deliveries to supply retailers with smaller amounts assembled and sorted to order.

Wide Area Network (WAN) *n.* A network spread over a large area such as a city or a country. May include a number of local area networks.

Wireless Markup Language (WML) *n.* A language that allows the text portions of web pages to be presented on wireless devices. WML is part of the Wireless Application Protocol (WAP) specification.

withdrawal of bid *n.* A bidder may withdraw a bid only if the request for withdrawal is received in the bid opening office prior to the time set

---

for opening the bids.

without prejudice *n.* Words used as a heading to a document or letter to indicate that what follows cannot be used in any way to harm an existing right or claim, cannot be taken as the signatory's last word, cannot bind the signatory in any way, and cannot be used as evidence in a court of law.

Won *n.* The standard monetary unit of North Korea and South Korea.

workflow *n.* A approval process that a requisition goes through before being sent to the supplier.

World Wide Web (WWW) *n.* An Internet system which makes use of the hyper-text markup language and hyper-text transfer protocol to store and distribute documents in a text form which are then interpreted by a browser program. The person is then shown the document with formatting, links, and graphics included.

WWW *n.* See World Wide Web (WWW).

Xx

X server *n.* A server of connections to X terminal's in a network that uses an X window system. An X server is typically installed in a UNIX-based operating system that allows the client to emulate the desktop environment of the server its connecting to.

X terminal *n.* A terminal especially designed to provide a user-interface for applications that run on a network's X server.

X Window system *n.* An open, cross-platform, client/server system for managing a windowed graphical user interface in a distributed network. Remote computers contain applications that make client requests for display management services in each workstation. It enables the user to see what the server would see if you were physically on that machine.

X12 *n.* An international standard for messages (EDI) developed by the Accredited Standards Committee (ASC) for ANSI.

XHTML *n.* The Extensible Hypertext Markup Language; the follow-on version of HTML 4. It can be extended (additional functionality) by anyone who uses it. New elements and attributes can be defined and added to those that already exist, making possible new ways to embed content and programming in a web page.

XML *n.* See extensible markup language (XML).

XML Query Language (XQL) *n.* A language used to locate and filter the elements and text in an XML document. XQL provides a tool for finding and/or selecting out specific items in the data collection in an XML file or set of files.

XPath *n.* A language that describes a way to locate and process items in XML documents by using an addressing syntax based on a path through the document's logical structure or hierarchy. This makes writing programming expressions easier than if each expression had to understand typical XML markup and its sequence in a document.

XPointer *n.* A language for locating data within an Extensible Markup Language (XML) document based on properties such as location within the document, character content, and attribute values.

XQL *n.* See XML Query Language (XQL).

XUL *n.* An acronym for Extensible User-Interface Language; A standard language used to exchange data that describes a program's user interface. One of the advantages of XUL is its simplicity. A few lines of XUL can accomplish what previously required many lines of code.

Yahoo *n.* A popular search engine on the World Wide Web.

Yen *n.* The standard monetary unit of Japan.

Yuan *n.* The standard monetary unit of the People's Republic of China.

yuppie *n.* A label for a successful or ambitious young person, especially one from the world of business. The word is formed from young upwardly-mobile professional.

Zz

zipping *v.* The process of packaging a set of files into a single file or archive that is called a zip file. Usually, the zip file is compressed so that they take up less space in storage or when sending to someone else. After receiving a zip file, you can uncompress and extract the original files before using them.

Zloty *n.* The standard monetary unit of Poland; its three character currency code is 'PLZ'.

zone pricing *v.* A pricing strategy in which a company delineates two or more zones. All the customers within a zone pay the same price for a product; the more distant the zone is from the company's headquarters or warehouse, the higher the price.

Appendix A

EDI TRANSACTION SET INDEX – ANSI X12

The ANSI X12 Transaction Index attempts to match the paper-based model of procurement, and standard EDI, which trading partners have traditionally used. Below are the common ANSI X12 EDI transaction sets for Electronic Commerce. Most EDI-enabled organizations will only use a small percentage of transaction set types, which usually fall in line with Industry standards. For example, most manufacturers trade 850's (Purchase Orders), 810's (Invoices), 832's (Catalog Feeds), 855's (Purchase Order Acknowledgements), 856's (Advanced Shipment Notices), 204's (Carrier Shipment Information), and 997's (Functional Acknowledgements). Of course, every organization has unique needs and may use significanly more. These transaction set types are common among most industries.

104 Air Shipment Information

110 Air Freight Details and Invoice

125 Multilevel Railcar Load Details

126 Vehicle Application Advice

127 Vehicle Baying Order

128 Dealer Information

129 Vehicle Carrier Rate Update

130 Student Educational Record (Transcript)

131 Student Educational Record (Transcript) Acknowledgment

135 Student Loan Application

139 Student Loan Guarantee Result

140 Product Registration

141 Product Service Claim Response

142 Product Service Claim

143 Product Service Notification

144 Student Loan Transfer and Status Verification

146 Request for Student Educational Record (Transcript)

147 Response to Request for Student Educational Record (Transcript)

148 Report of Injury or Illness

151 Electronic Filing of Tax Return Data Acknowledgment

152 Statistical Government Information

271 Health Care Eligibility/Benefit Information

272 Property and Casualty Loss Notification

276 Health Care Claim Status Request

277 Health Care Claim Status Notification

290 Cooperative Advertising Agreements

300 Reservation (Booking Request) (Ocean)

301 Confirmation (Ocean)

303 Booking Cancellation (Ocean)

304 Shipping Instructions

309 U.S. Customs Manifest

310 Freight Receipt and Invoice (Ocean)

311 Canadian Customs Information

312 Arrival Notice (Ocean)

313 Shipment Status Inquiry (Ocean)

315 Status Details (Ocean)

317 Delivery/Pickup Order

319 Terminal Information

322 Terminal Operations Activity (Ocean)

323 Vessel Schedule and Itinerary (Ocean)

324 Vessel Stow Plan (Ocean)

325 Consolidation of Goods In Container

326 Consignment Summary List

350 U.S. Customs Release Information

352 U.S. Customs Carrier General Order Status

353 U.S. Customs Events Advisory Details

354 U.S. Customs Automated Manifest Archive Status

355 U.S. Customs Manifest Acceptance/Rejection

356 Permit To Transfer Request

361 Carrier Interchange Agreement (Ocean)

404 Rail Carrier Shipment Information

410 Rail Carrier Freight Details and Invoice

414 Rail Carrier Settlements

417 Rail Carrier Waybill Interchange

418 Rail Advance Interchange Consist

419 Advance Car Disposition

420 Car Handling Information

421 Estimated Time of Arrival and Car Scheduling

422 Shipper's Car Order

425 Rail Waybill Request

426 Rail Revenue Waybill

429 Railroad Retirement Activity

431 Railroad Station Master File

440 Shipment Weights

466 Rate Request

468 Rate Docket Journal Log

485 Ratemaking Action

490 Rate Group Definition

492 Miscellaneous Rates

494 Scale Rate Table

511 Requisition

517 Material Obligation Validation

527 Material Due-In and Receipt

536 Logistics Reassignment

561 Contract Abstract

567 Contract Completion Status

---

568 Contract Payment Management Report

601 Shipper's Export Declaration

602 Transportation Services Tender

622 Intermodal Ramp Activity

805 Contract Pricing Proposal

806 Project Schedule Reporting

810 Invoice

811 Consolidated Service Invoice/Statement

812 Credit/Debit Adjustment

813 Electronic Filing of Tax Return Data

815 Cryptographic Service Message

816 Organizational Relationships

818 Commission Sales Report

819 Operating Expense Statement

820 Payment Order/Remittance Advice

821 Financial Information Reporting

822 Customer Account Analysis

823 Lockbox

824 Application Advice

---

826 Tax Information Reporting

827 Financial Return Notice

828 Debit Authorization

829 Payment Cancellation Request

830 Planning Schedule with Release Capability

831 Application Control Totals

832 Price/Sales Catalog

833 Residential Mortgage Credit Report Order

834 Benefit Enrollment and Maintenance

835 Health Care Claim Payment/Advice

836 Contract Award

837 Health Care Claim

838 Trading Partner Profile

839 Project Cost Reporting

840 Request for Quotation

841 Specifications/Technical Information

842 Nonconformance Report

843 Response to Request for Quotation

---

844 Product Transfer Account Adjustment

845 Price Authorization Acknowledgment/Status

846 Inventory Inquiry/Advice

847 Material Claim

848 Material Safety Data Sheet

849 Response to Product Transfer Account Adjustment

850 Purchase Order

851 Asset Schedule

852 Product Activity Data

853 Routing and Carrier Instruction

854 Shipment Delivery Discrepancy Information

855 Purchase Order Acknowledgment

856 Ship Notice/Manifest

857 Shipment and Billing Notice

858 Shipment Information

859 Freight Invoice

860 Purchase Order Change Request - Buyer Initiated

861 Receiving Advice/Acceptance Certificate

862 Shipping Schedule

863 Report of Test Results

864 Text Message

865 Purchase Order Change Acknowledgment/Request - Seller Initiated

866 Production Sequence

867 Product Transfer and Resale Report

868 Electronic Form Structure

869 Order Status Inquiry

870 Order Status Report

872 Residential Mortgage Insurance Application

875 Grocery Products Purchase Order

876 Grocery Products Purchase Order Change

878 Product Authorization/Deauthorization

879 Price Change

880 Grocery Products Invoice

882 Direct Store Delivery Summary Information

888 Item Maintenance

889 Promotion Announcement

893 Item Information Request

894 Delivery/Return Base Record

895 Delivery/Return Acknowledgment or Adjustment

896 Product Dimension Maintenance

920 Loss or Damage Claim - General Commodities

924 Loss or Damage Claim - Motor Vehicle

925 Claim Tracer

926 Claim Status Report and Tracer Reply

928 Automotive Inspection Detail

940 Warehouse Shipping Order

943 Warehouse Stock Transfer Shipment Advice

944 Warehouse Stock Transfer Receipt Advice

945 Warehouse Shipping Advice

947 Warehouse Inventory Adjustment Advice

980 Functional Group Totals

990 Response to a Load Tender

996 File Transfer

997 Functional Acknowledgment

998 Set Cancellation

Appendix B

EDIFACT MESSAGES

EDIFACT is a set of internationally agreed standards to conduct electronic interchange of business documents. The idea and purpose of EDIFACT is almost identical to ANSI X12 EDI (implemented in North America), but is used primarily in Europe. The messages below are the equivalent to the ANSI X12 Transaction Set numbers presented in Appendix A.

A

APERAK Application error and acknowledgement message

AUTHOR Authorization message

AVLREQ Availability request - Interactive message

AVLRSP Availability response - Interactive message

B

BALANC Trail Balance

BANSTA Banking status message

BAPLIE Bayplan/stowage plan - occupied and empty locations message

BAPLTE Bayplan/stowage plan - total numbers message

BOPBNK Bank transactions and portfolio transactions report

BOPCUS Balance of payment customer transaction report

BOPDIR Direct balance of payment declaration message

BOPINF Balance of payment information from customer message

BOPSTA Exchange of balance of payment statistics

C

CALINF Vessel call information message

CASINT Request for legal administration action in civil proceedings message

CASRES Legal administration response in civil proceedings message

CHACCO Chart of accounts

CLAREQ Classification general request

CLASET Classification information set

COACOR Container acceptance order

COACSU Commercial account summary

COARCO Container arrival confirmation

COARIN Container arrival information

COARNO Container arrival notice

COARRI Container discharge/loading report

CODECO Container gate-in/gate-out report

CODENO Permit expiration/clearance ready notice

CODEPA Container departure message

COEDOR Container stock report

COHAOR Container special handling order

COITON Container inland transport order notice

COITOR Container inland transport order

COITOS Container inland transport order response

COITSR Container inland transport space request

COLADV Advice of a documentary collection

COLREQ Request for a documentary collection

COMCON Component parts content message

COMDIS Commercial dispute message

CONAPW Advice on pending works message

CONDPV Direct payment valuation message

CONDRA Drawing administration message

CONDRO Drawing organisation message

CONEST Establishment of contract message

CONITT Invitation to tender message

CONPVA Payment valuation message

CONQVA Quantity valuation message

CONRPW Response of pending works

CONTEN Tender message

CONWQD Work item quantity determination message

COOVLA Container overlanded message

COPARN Container announcement message

COPAYM Contributions for payment message

COPDEM Container predeparture with guidelines message

COPINF Container pick-up information

COPINO Container pre-notification message

COPRAR Container discharge/loading order message

COPRDP Container predeparture message

COREOR Container release order

COSHLA Container shortlanded message

COSTCO Container stuffing/stripping confirmation

COSTOR Container stuffing/stripping order

CREADV Credit advice message

CREEXT Extended credit advice message

CREMUL Multiple credit advice message

CURRAC Current account message

CUSCAR Customs cargo report

CUSDEC Customs declaration message

CUSEXP Customs express consignment declaration message

CUSPED Periodic customs declaration message

CUSREP Customs conveyance report message

CUSRES Customs response message

D

DEBADV Debit advice message

DEBMUL Multiple debit advice message

DELFOR Delivery schedule message

DELJIT Delivery just in time message

DESADV Despatch advice message

DESTIM Equipment damage and repair estimate message

DGRECA Dangerous goods recapitulation message

DIRDEB Direct debit message

DIRDEF Directory definition message

DOCADV Documentary credit advice message

DOCAMA Advice of an amendment of a documentary credit

DOCAMD Direct amendment of a documentary credit

DOCAMI Documentary credit amendment information

DOCAMR Request for an amendment of a documentary credit

DOCAPP Documentary credit application message

DOCARE Response to an amendment of a documentary credit

DOCINF Documentary credit issuance information

DOCISD Direct documentary credit issuance

DOCTRD Direct transfer of a documentary credit

DOCTRI Documentary credit transfer information

DOCTRR Request to transfer a documentary credit

E

ENTREC Accounting entries message

F

FINCAN Financial cancellation message

FINPAY Multiple interbank funds transfer message

FINSTA Financial statement of an account message

FUNACK Functional acknowledgement

G

GATEAC Gate and intermodal ramp activities message

GENRAL General purpose message

GESMES Generic statistical message

H

HANMOV Cargo/goods handling and movement message

I

ICASRQ Loss assessment request message

ICNOMO Insurance claims notification message

IFCSUM Forwarding and consolidation summary message

IFTCCA Forwarding and transport shipment charge calculation message

IFTDGN Dangerous goods notification message

IFTFCC International freight costs and other charges message

IFTIAG Dangerous cargo list message

IFTMAN Arrival notice message

IFTMBC Booking confirmation message

IFTMBF Firm booking message

IFTMBP Provisional booking message

IFTMCS Instruction contract status message

IFTMIN Instruction message

IFTRIN Forwarding and transport rate information message

IFTSAI Forwarding and transport schedule and availability information message

IFTSTA International multimodal status report message

IFTSTQ International multimodal status request

IMPDEF EDI Implementation guideline definition message

INFENT Enterprise information

INSDES Instruction to dispatch message

INSPRE Insurance premium message

INVOIC Invoice message

INVRPT Inventory report

IPPOMO Motor insurance policy message

ITRGRP In transit groupage message

ITRRPT In transit report detail message

J

JAPRES Job application result message

JIBILL Joint interest billing report message

JINFDE Job information demand message

JOBAPP Job application proposal message

JOBCON Job order confirmation message

JOBMOD Job order modification message

JOBOFF Job order message

L

LREACT Life insurance activity message

M

MEDADR Medical adverse drug reaction message

MEDPID Person identification message

MEDPRE Medical prescription message

MEDREQ Medical service request message

MEDRPT Medical service report message

MEDRUC Medical resource usage/cost message

MEQPOS Means of transport and equipment position message

MOVINS Stowage instruction message

MSCONS Metered services consumption report

O

ORDCHG Purchase order change request message

ORDERS Purchase order message

ORDRSP Purchase order response message

OSTENQ Order status enquiry message

OSTRPT Order status report

P

PARTIN Party information message (Trading partner profile data)

PAXLST Passenger list message

PAYDUC Payroll deductions advice message

PAYEXT Extended payment order message

PAYMUL Multiple payment order message

PAYORD Payment order message

PRDSRC Product source information message

PRICAT Price/sales catalogue message

PRIHIS Pricing history message

PRODAT Product data message

PRODEX Product exchange reconciliation message

PROINQ Product inquiry message

PROTAP Project tasks planning message

PRPAID Insurance premium payment message

Q

QALITY Quality data message

QLSPEC Specification message

QUOTES Quote message

R

RDRMES Raw data reporting message

REACTR Equipment reservation, release, acceptance and termination message

REBORD Reinsurance bordereau message

RECADV Receiving advice message

RECALC Reinsurance calculation message

RECECO Credit risk cover message

RECLAM Reinsurance claims message

REGENT Registration of enterprise message

REINAC Reinsurance account message

REMADV Remittance advice message

REPREM Reinsurance premium message

REQDOC Request for document message

REQOTE Request for quote message

RESETT Reinsurance settlement message

RESMSG Reservation message

RESREQ Reservation request - Interactive message

RESRSP Reservation response - Interactive message

RETACC Reinsurance technical account message

RETANN Announcement for returns message

RETINS Instruction for returns message

S

SAFHAZ Safety and hazard data message

SANCRT International movement of goods governmental regulatory message

SLSFCT Sales forecast message

SLSRPT Sales data report message

SOCADE Social administration declaration

SSIMOD Modification of identity details message

SSRECH Worker's insurance history message

SSREGW Notification of registration of a worker

STATAC Statement of account message

STLRPT Settlement transaction reporting message

SUPCOT Superannuation contributions advice message

SUPMAN Superannuation maintenance message

SUPRES Supplier response message (Reservation response message)

T

TANSTA Tank status report message

TAXCON Tax control message

TESTEX Test message explicit mode

TESTIM Test message implicit mode

TINREQ Tourism information request message

TINRSP Tourism information response message

TRADES Traffic or travel description definition message

TRADIN Traffic or travel details of individual traveller message

TRAILS Traffic or travel route guidance and planning message

TRALOC Traffic or travel location definition message

TRAREQ Traffic or travel information request message

TRAVAK Traffic or travel information acknowledgement message

TRAVIN Traffic or travel situation information message

V

VATDEC Value added tax message

VESDEP Vessel departure message

W

WASDIS Waste disposal information message

WKGRDC Work grant decision message

WKGRRE Work grant request message

Appendix C

COUNTRY CURRENCY CODES

This is a list of global currencies and the three-character currency code used to represent them. Often, but not always, this code is the same as the ISO 4217 standard. (The ISO -- or International Organization for Standardization -- is a worldwide federation of national standards bodies.) In most cases, the ISO 4217 currency code is composed of the country's two-character ISO 3166 country code plus an extra character to denote the currency unit. For example, the code for Canadian Dollars is simply Canada's two-character ISO 3166 code ("CA") plus a one-character currency designator ("D"). Be aware that countries that converted to the Euro is not reflected here.

Sorted by Country, Currency Name, and Code.

A

Afghanistan Afghani, AFA
Albania Lek, ALL
Algeria Algerian Dinar, DZD
America (United States of America), US Dollar, USD
American Samoa US Dollar, USD

American Virgin Islands US Dollar, USD
Andorra French Franc, FRF
Andorra Spanish Peseta, ESP
Angola New Kwanza, AON
Anguilla East Caribbean Dollar, XCD
Antigua and Barbuda East Caribbean Dollar, XCD
Argentina Peso, ARP
Armenia Dram, AMD
Aruba Florin, AWF
Australia Dollar, AUD
Austria Schilling, ATS
Azerbaijan Manat, AZM
Azores Portuguese Escudo, PTE

B

Bahamas Dollar, BSD
Bahrain Dinar, BHD
Baleares (Balearic Islands) Spanish Peseta, ESP
Bangladesh Taka, BDT
Barbados Dollar, BBD
Barbuda and Antigua East Caribbean Dollar, XCD
Belarus Ruble, BYR
Belgium Franc, BEF
Belize Dollar, BZD
Benin CFA Franc, XAF
Bermuda Dollar, BMD
Bhutan Indian Rupee, INR
Bhutan Rupee, BTR
Bolivia Boliviano, BOB
Bonaire Netherlands Antilles Guilder, ANG
Bosnia and Herzegovina Convertible Mark, BAK
Botswana Pula, BWP
Bouvet Island Norwegian Krone, NOK

Brazil Brazilian Real, BRL
Britain (Great Britain) Pound Sterling, GBP
British Indian Ocean Territory US Dollar, USD
British Virgin Islands US Dollar, USD
Brunei Darussalam Dollar, BND
Bulgaria Lev, BGL
Burkina Faso CFA Franc, XAF
Burma (Myanmar) Kyat, MMK
Burundi Burundi Franc, BIF

C

Côte D'Ivoire CFA Franc, XAF
Caicos and Turks Islands US Dollar, USD
Cambodia Riel, KHR
Cameroon CFA Franc, XAF
Canada Dollar, CAD
Canary Islands Spanish Peseta, ESP
Cape Verde Escudo, CVE
Cayman Islands Dollar, KYD
Central African Republic CFA Franc, XAF
Chad CFA Franc, XAF
Chile Peso, CLP
China Yuan Renminbi, CNY
Christmas Island Australian Dollar, AUD
Cocos (Keeling) Islands Australian Dollar, AUD
Colombia Peso, COP
Comoros Franc, KMF
Communauté Financière Africaine CFA Franc, XAF
Congo-Brazzaville CFA Franc, XAF
Congo-Kinshasa Congolese Franc, CDF
Cook Islands New Zealand Dollar, NZD
Costa Rica Colon, CRC
Croatia Kuna, HRK

Cuba Peso, CUP
Curaço Netherlands Antilles Guilder, ANG
Cyprus Pound, CYP
Czech Republic Koruna, CZK

D

Denmark Krone, DKK
Djibouti Franc, DJF
Dominica East Caribbean Dollar, XCD
Dominican Republic Peso, DOP
Dutch (The Netherlands) Guilder, NLG

E

East Caribbean Dollar, XCD
East Timor Indonesian Rupiah, IDR
Ecuador Sucre, ECS
Egypt Pound, EGP
Eire (Ireland) Punt, IEP
El Salvador Colon, SVC
EMU (European Economic and Monetary Union) Euro, EUR
England (Great Britain) Pound Sterling, GBP
Equatorial Guinea CFA Franc, XAF
Eritrea Ethiopian Birr, ETB
Eritrea Nakfa, ERN
Estonia Kroon, EEK
Ethiopia Birr, ETB
European Union Euro, EUR
European Economic and Monetary Union (EMU) Euro, EUR

F

Falkland Islands (Malvinas) Pound, FKP
Faroe Islands Danish Krone, DKK
Fiji Dollar, FJD
Finland Markka, FIM
France Franc, FRF
French Guiana French Franc, FRF
French Pacific Islands (French Polynesia) CFP Franc, XPF
French Polynesia (French Pacific Islands) CFP Franc, XPF
French Southern Territories French Franc, FRF
Futuna and Wallis Islands CFP Franc, XPF

G

Gabon CFA Franc, XAF
Gambia Dalasi, GMD
Georgia Lari, GEL
Germany Deutsche Mark, DEM
Ghana Cedi, GHC
Gibraltar Pound, GIP
Gold Ounces, XAU
Great Britain Pound Sterling, GBP
Greece Drachma, GRD
Greenland Danish Krone, DKK
Grenada East Caribbean Dollar, XCD
Grenadines and Saint Vincent East Caribbean Dollar, XCD
Guadeloupe French Franc, FRF
Guam US Dollar, USD
Guatemala Quetzal, GTQ
Guinea Franc, GNF
Guinea-Bissau CFA Franc, XAF
Guyana Dollar, GYD

H

Haiti Gourde, HTG
Haiti US Dollar, USD
Heard Island and McDonald Islands Australian Dollar, AUD
Herzegovina and Bosnia Convertible Mark, BAK
Holland (The Netherlands) Guilder, NLG
Honduras Lempira, HNL
Hong Kong Dollar, HKD
Hungary Forint, HUF

I

International Monetary Fund (IMF) Special Drawing Right, XDR
Iceland Krona, ISK
India Rupee, INR
Indonesia Rupiah, IDR
Iran Rial, IRR
Iraq Dinar, IQD
Ireland (Eire) Punt, IEP
Israel Shekel, ILS
Italy Lira, ITL
Ivory Coast CFA Franc, XAF

J

Jamaica Dollar, JMD
Jan Mayen and Svalbard Norwegian Krone, NOK
Japan Yen, JPY

Jordan Dinar, JOD

K

Kazakstan Tenge, KZT
Keeling (Cocos) Islands Australian Dollar, AUD
Kenya Shilling, KES
Kiribati Australian Dollar, AUD
Korea (North) Won, KPW
Korea (South) Won, KRW
Kuwait Dinar, KWD
Kyrgyzstan Som, KGS

L

Laos Kip, LAK
Latvia Lat, LVL
Lebanon Pound, LBP
Lesotho Loti, LSL
Lesotho South African Rand, ZAR
Liberia Dollar, LRD
Libya Dinar, LYD
Liechtenstein Swiss Franc, CHF
Lithuania Lita, LTL
Luxembourg Franc, LUF

M

Macau Pataca, MOP
Macedonia Denar, MKD

Madagascar Malagasy Franc, MGF
Madeira Islands Portuguese Escudo, PTE
Malawi Kwacha, MWK
Malaysia Ringgit, MYR
Maldives (Maldive Islands) Rufiyaa, MVR
Mali CFA Franc, XAF
Malta Lira, MTL
Malvinas (Falkland Islands) Pound, FKP
Mariana Islands (Northern) US Dollar, USD
Marshall Islands US Dollar, USD
Martinique French Franc, FRF
Mauritania Ouguiya, MRO
Mauritius Rupee, MUR
Mayotte French Franc, FRF
McDonald Islands and Heard Island Australian Dollar, AUD
Mexico Peso, MXP
Micronesia (Federated States of) US Dollar, USD
Midway Islands US Dollar, USD
Miquelon and Saint Pierre French Franc, FRF
Moldova Leu, MDL
Monaco French Franc, FRF
Mongolia Tugrik, MNT
Montenegro and Serbia Yugoslav New Dinar, YUN
Montserrat East Caribbean Dollar, XCD
Morocco Dirham, MAD
Mozambique Metical, MZM
Myanmar (Burma) Kyat, MMK

N

Namibia Dollar, NAD
Namibia South African Rand, ZAR
Nauru Australian Dollar, AUD
Nepal Nepalese Rupee, NPR

Netherlands (The) Guilder, NLG
Netherlands Antilles Guilder, ANG
Nevis and Saint Kitts East Caribbean Dollar, XCD
New Caledonia CFP Franc, XPF
New Zealand Dollar, NZD
Nicaragua Cordoba Oro, NIO
Niger CFA Franc, XAF
Nigeria Naira, NGN
Niue New Zealand Dollar, NZD
Norfolk Island Australian Dollar, AUD
Northern Mariana Islands US Dollar, USD
Norway Krone, NOK

O

Oman Sul Rial, OMR

P

Pakistan Rupee, PKR
Palau US Dollar, USD
Panama Balboa, PAB
Panama US Dollar, USD
Papua New Guinea Kina, PGK
Paraguay Guarani, PYG
Peru Nuevo Sol, PEN
Philippines Peso, PHP
Pitcairn Islands New Zealand Dollar, NZD
Platinum Ounces, XPT
Poland Zloty, PLZ
Portugal Escudo, PTE
Principe and São Tome Dobra, STD

Puerto Rico US Dollar, USD

Q

Qatar Rial, QAR

R

Réunion French Franc, FRF
Romania Leu, ROL
Russia Ruble, RUR
Rwanda Rwanda Franc, RWF

S

São Tome and Principe Dobra, STD
Saba Netherlands Antilles Guilder, ANG
Sahara (Western) Moroccan Dirham, MAD
Saint Christopher East Caribbean Dollar, XCD
Saint Helena Pound, SHP
Saint Kitts and Nevis East Caribbean Dollar, XCD
Saint Lucia East Caribbean Dollar, XCD
Saint Pierre and Miquelon French Franck, FRF
Saint Vincent and The Grenadines East Caribbean Dollar, XCD
Saint-Martin French Francs, FRF
Samoa (American) US Dollar, USD
Samoa (Western) Tala, WST
San Marino Italian Lira, ITL
Saudi Arabia Riyal, SAR
Seborga Luigino, SBL

Senegal CFA Franc, XAF
Serbia and Montenegro Yugoslav New Dinar, YUN
Seychelles Rupee, SCR
Sierra Leone Leone, SLL
Singapore Dollar, SGD
Sint Eustatius Netherlands Antilles Guilder, ANG
Sint Maarten Netherlands Antilles Guilder, ANG
Slovakia Koruna, SKK
Slovenia Tolar, SIT
Solomon Islands Dollar, SBD
Somalia Shilling, SOS
South Africa Rand, ZAR
South Georgia British Pounds, GBP
South Sandwich Islands British Pounds, GBP
Spain Peseta, ESP
Special Drawing Right XDR
Sri Lanka Rupee, LKR
Sudan Dinar, SDD
Suriname Guilder, SRG
Svalbard and Jan Mayen Norwegian Krone, NOK
Swaziland Lilangeni, SZL
Sweden Krona, SEK
Switzerland Franc, CHF
Syria Pound, SYP

T

Taiwan Dollar, TWD
Tajikistan Ruble, TJR
Tajikistan Russian Ruble, RUR
Tanzania Shilling, TZS
Thailand Baht, THB
Timor (East) Indonesian Rupiah, IDR
Tobago and Trinidad Dollar, TTD

Togo CFA Franc, XAF
Tokelau New Zealand Dollar, NZD
Tonga Pa'anga, TOP
Trinidad and Tobago Dollar, TTD
Tunisia Dinar, TND
Turkey Lira, TRL
Turkmenistan Manat, TMM
Turks and Caicos Islands US Dollar, USD
Tuvalu Australian Dollar, AUD

U

US Virgin Islands US Dollar, USD
Uganda Shilling, UGX
Ukraine Hryvnia, UAH
United Arab Emirates Dirham, AED
United Kingdom (Great Britain) Pound Sterling, GBP
United States Minor Outlying Islands US Dollar, USD
United States of America US Dollar, USD
Uruguay Peso, UYU
Uzbekistan Som, UZS

V

Vanuatu Vatu, VUV
Vatican City (The Holy See) Italian Lira, ITL
Venezuela Bolivar, VEB
Viet Nam Dong, VND
Virgin Islands (American) US Dollar, USD
Virgin Islands (British) US Dollar, USD

W

Wake Island US Dollar, USD
Wallis and Futuna Islands CFP Franc, XPF
West Samoa Tala, WST
Western Sahara Moroccan Dirham, MAD
Western Samoa Tala, WST

Y

Yemen Rial, YER
Yugoslavia New Dinar, YUN

Z

Zambia Kwacha, ZMK
Zimbabwe Zimbabwe Dollar, ZWD

	DATE DUE		
JUN 0 1 2005			